THE LIGHTHOUSE

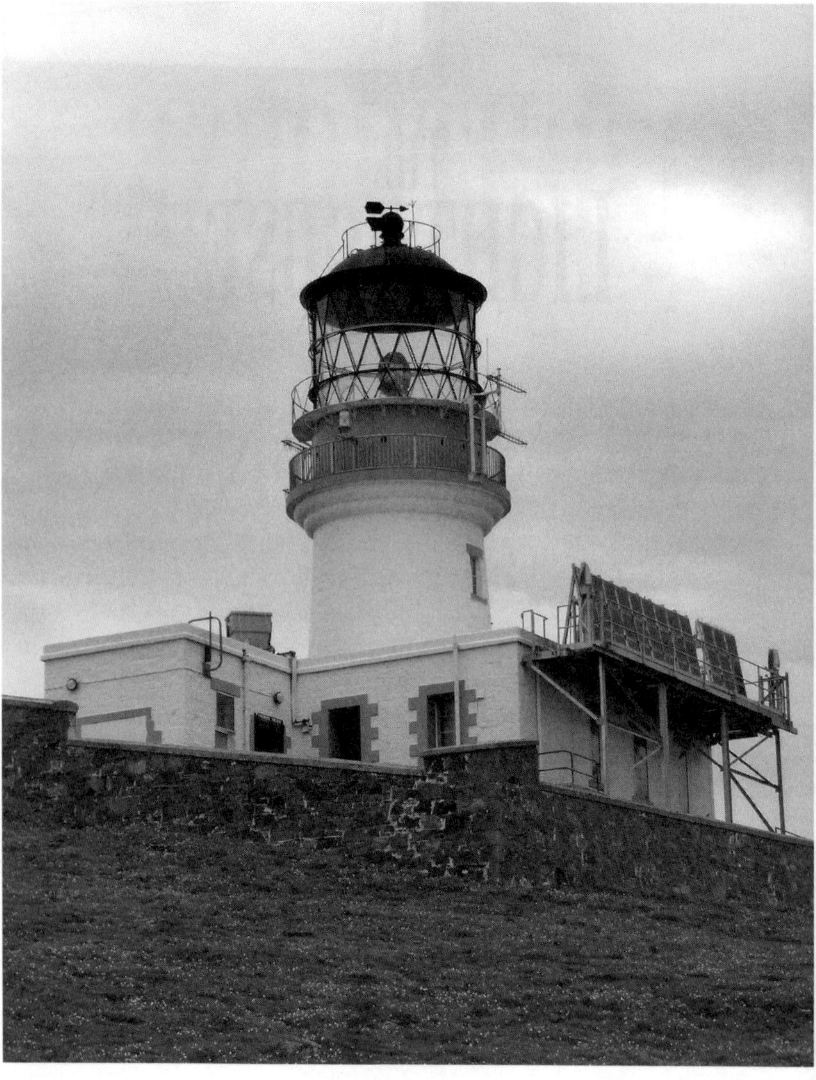

THE LIGHTHOUSE

THE MYSTERY OF THE EILEAN MOR LIGHTHOUSE KEEPERS

KEITH McCLOSKEY

The History Press

In Memory of Calum Eric Macaulay Sutherland 1952–2009.
A Lewisman at Heart.

Cover: Lighthouse in mist. (Robert Llewellyn / Alamy). *Frontispiece:* The lighthouse as it is today – apart from one or two modern additions (solar panels), basically unchanged from December 1900. (Chris Downer)

First published 2014

The History Press
The Mill, Brimscombe Port
Stroud, Gloucestershire, GL5 2QG
www.thehistorypress.co.uk

© Keith McCloskey 2014

The right of Keith McCloskey to be identified as the Author
of this work has been asserted in accordance with the
Copyright, Designs and Patents Act 1988.

All rights reserved. No part of this book may be reprinted
or reproduced or utilised in any form or by any electronic,
mechanical or other means, now known or hereafter invented,
including photocopying and recording, or in any information
storage or retrieval system, without the permission in writing
from the Publishers.

British Library Cataloguing in Publication Data.
A catalogue record for this book is available from the British Library.

ISBN 978 0 7509 5365 8

Typesetting and origination by The History Press
Printed in Great Britain

Contents

Foreword		7
Acknowledgements		9
Prologue: The Missing Light		11
1	Lewis and the Flannans	15
2	The NLB and the Life of a Lighthouseman	21
3	The Lightkeepers and a Reconstruction of 15 December 1900	55
4	Discovery	65
5	Aftermath	89
6	Giant Wave	119
7	Murder	147
8	Supernatural	173
9	Conclusions	197
Appendix I: 'Flannan Isle'		201
Appendix II: Abstract of Signalman's Returns (Roderick MacKenzie) for Flannan Isles Lighthouse		205
Appendix III: Weather Details		207
Appendix IV: Recollections of the Eilean Mor Lighthouse by Norrie Muir PLK		211
Appendix V: Eilean Mor Lighthouse Prayer		215
Sources and Further Reading		217
Index		219

Foreword

I was intrigued by the story of the missing lighthousemen on Eilean Mor for many years, particularly as good friends of mine lived in Carloway. It is a tragedy which has been debated constantly by those interested in mysteries of the sea. There is plenty of information within books, magazines, newspaper archives and the internet about the story but once I delved into them, numerous inaccuracies cropped up. For instance, one of the biggest misconceptions of this story is the state of the sea and the weather at the Flannan Isles on the 15 December 1900. It is generally believed that the sea was relatively calm and the weather was not unduly 'bad'. The records show that this is not the case, however.

What I want to do in this book is to present all the facts to the reader and let them make their own minds up after looking at the evidence. The giant wave theory is almost too obvious, but using the principle of *Occam's Razor* it is possibly the correct answer as to what happened. Having spent a considerable amount of time looking into this mystery I have to say I am not entirely convinced by the most obvious answer for reasons I give in the text, but as I said, it is up to the reader to draw their own conclusions.

I would also like to say that produced in this book is the first published photograph of what is believed to be the three missing men together, which was kindly provided to me by Steven Gibbons, a relative of Thomas Marshall.

The following description was given to me by a former Northern Lighthouse Board (NLB) lighthouse keeper: 'We were ordinary folk, doing a job that was far from ordinary.' With this in mind, I have tried to introduce brief aspects of the life of a lighthouse keeper for the reader to understand a little about their lives. The terms lighthouse keeper, lightkeeper and keeper are all interchangeable.

Keith McCloskey
Berkshire
January 2014

Acknowledgements

I would like to acknowledge the kind assistance of the following: Lorna Hunter and the NLB; Colin Sutherland, Lord Carloway; Norrie Simpson for additional research; Arthur Flynn; Sheila Ryan for permission to use her research material; Anne Cowne of Lloyds Register Group Services Ltd; Mark Beswick of the Meteorological Office National Meteorological Archive, Exeter; Professor Elizabeth Austin of Edinburgh University; Judy Greenway and the Trustees of the Wilfrid Wilson Gibson Estate; Ian Cowe for the use of his photo of the shore station at Breasclete; Chris Downer for the use of his excellent photos; Christopher Nicholson; Sigurd Towrie for permission to use his Stronsay Beast article on the Orkneyjar website as source material; Jay C. Buckey Jr MD; Robert Stewart, retired Professor of Oceanography at Texas A&M University; Yvonne Shand at the National Library of Scotland; Merrilyn MacAulay and Donnie G. Macleod, Catherine Mackie Quirk and Ian Begg for information relating to her great grandfather PLK William Beggs; Iain Macaulay for his very helpful information and advice; Iain Angus for his description of the *Muir Cul*; the very helpful staff of Seatrek who run trips out to the Flannans and St Kilda; Triona McCloskey, Camilla McCloskey and Marcella O'Sullivan for proofreading; also Liz Turner and Morag Mcfadden for use of their photos.

A special mention for former NLB keepers Alistair Henderson, Ron Ireland (also thanks for use of Ron's Flannans photographs) and Norrie Muir. Both Ron Ireland and Norrie Muir have served on the Flannan Isles Lighthouse.

A very special mention also to Steven Gibbons for allowing me to use the photos of Thomas Marshall and to Hugo Mander for drawing my attention to them.

I am especially grateful to Alistair Henderson for his considerable input and advice.

PROLOGUE: THE MISSING LIGHT

Approaching midnight on the night of 15–16 December 1900, approximately 80 miles out north-west from the Scottish mainland in the North Atlantic, a 2,193-ton cargo vessel made her way through the dark, cold waters. The vessel was the SS *Archtor*, registered in London with a crew of twenty-four and jointly owned by Francis Arthur Holman and others, carrying general cargo from Philadelphia in the USA to Leith. The *Archtor* had originally been launched five years earlier as the SS *Whetstone* and had been renamed *Archtor* only a year previously. It was a regular, even mundane, run between the two ports for the vessel, although the weather had been stormy for most of the voyage. The severity of the storm had swept away one of the four compasses that she carried from her poop deck. Despite the weather having settled down somewhat, there was still a very heavy swell[1] and the *Archtor* struggled to make a constant speed of 10 knots, its indicated speed, even though the storm had abated. At this point she was less than two days sailing away from Leith, the port for Edinburgh. At mid-afternoon that day (15 December 1900), the ship's position had been 58° 29' N and 11° 36' W, approximately 120 miles west by north from the Flannan Islands.[2]

As the evening came on and the *Archtor* approached the Flannan Islands, the master of the vessel, Captain Holman, felt that something was not right. Despite searching constantly on the horizon as they came closer to the islands, there was only darkness, and even though there was a very heavy sea with a strong south-south-westerly wind, it was a clear night.

By midnight, the *Archtor* had reached a point that was estimated to be well within 5 miles to the north of the Flannan Islands and the relatively new lighthouse.[3] Even with the changeover of watches at midnight there was still no sighting of the light. Once again, Captain Holman stood on the bridge and scanned the horizon to the south to search for the light from the Flannan Islands lighthouse, which had only been in operation for a year. The lighthouse itself had officially become operational on 7 December 1899 and had been built on the largest of the Flannan Islands, named Eilean Mor. Depending on the weather and visibility, the light had a range of up to 24 miles.

As the vessel got closer and came well within range of the light, there was still only darkness and the *Archtor* passed through the area without any sighting of it. The *Archtor* continued steering on a south-east by east course until 4 a.m. on the morning of 16 December,[4] then altered course slightly to take the ship to the Butt of Lewis, which they reached at 7 a.m. that morning. The non-appearance of the light perturbed Captain Holman and he made another quick calculation based on the position of the ship on a bearing east by south and a distance of 16 miles, and he concluded that they had certainly passed within 6 miles of the Flannan Islands and Eilean Mor Lighthouse, which altered his earlier figure of passing within 5 miles. He had also failed to see the landmass of the Flannan Islands, which they were trying to make out as a 'landfall'. The failure to observe the islands themselves was of little consequence but the complete absence of the light was a more worrying issue. Nevertheless, he resolved to report the matter on arrival at Leith. There would, however, be a delay in Captain Holman reporting the non-operation of the Eilean Mor Lighthouse, as the *Archtor* was to run into a serious problem of her own within forty-eight hours of passing the Flannan Islands.[5]

As Captain Holman searched in vain for the light, he would not have known at that point, 20 miles to the south-east of the Flannan Islands, that there was another potential observer who could have shared his concerns about the non-appearance of the light over a number of days. The Northern Lighthouse Board (NLB) paid a gamekeeper, Roderick MacKenzie, on Lewis, the sum of £8 a year to act as an observer to the light. Lewis is the largest of the Outer Hebrides islands and the nearest point to the Flannan Islands. Roderick Mackenzie made his observations of the light from Gallan Head on Lewis where principally he was to keep an eye out for any signals from the Eilean Mor Lighthouse. He was specifically tasked to watch for signals from the lighthouse as opposed to any non-operation of the light itself. Any problems connected with the operation of the light would then be communicated to him through signals which he could then act on. If he observed any signals indicating a problem of any nature, he was required to send a telegram to the Head Office of the Northern Lighthouse Board (NLB) in Edinburgh immediately informing them. The NLB could then arrange for any repairs to be made as soon as possible.[6] Roderick Mackenzie had last noted the light was operating on 7 December 1900 and had not seen it since that date. One week and one day later, on 15 December 1900, he had still not seen the light, but he put this down to the appalling weather and atmospheric conditions at the time. He had on previous occasions not observed the light for days at a time due to bad weather and thought nothing more of it, provided he saw no signals during the day and provided he saw the light eventually after a short period of a few days. After 15 December had come and gone and the days got closer to Christmas, Mackenzie asked both of his sons to assist him in keeping a watch towards the Flannans, as he was by now starting to get worried at the length of time it had been since he had seen the light.

Notwithstanding Captain Holman's concerns – and the fact that Roderick Mackenzie would have been primarily looking for daytime signals rather than a light working at night – it was a possibility that, as the light had only become operational a year previously, a few teething problems could occur. However with the passing of a year, it would not be expected that the light would fail over a period of several days. Nevertheless, the non-appearance of the light over such a period would have been considered a very serious matter. Before anybody set out to the islands, no one would have suspected that a major tragedy had taken place.

Notes
1 Captain Holman's statement 29 December 1900 of passing the Flannan Isles on 15–16 December 1900, Scottish National Archives File NLC3/1/1.
2 Ibid.
3 Ibid.
4 Ibid.
5 She hit the Carphie Rock, see Chapter 4.
6 Scottish National Archives File NLC3/1/1.

1

LEWIS AND THE FLANNANS

The history and folklore of the Outer Hebrides is inextricably linked to the sea. Situated off the north-west coast of mainland Scotland, the islands have a remoteness that can give a feeling of isolation which helps the reader to appreciate the life of the people who have lived and worked here, leading hard and unrelenting lives. In terms of the lighthouses, this isolation is amplified and it can be said that the lighthouse on Eilean Mor is a lonely and remote place in what is already considered to be an isolated area.

An understanding of the folklore lends background to one of the more outlandish theories (*see Chapter 8*) concerning the disappearance of the lighthousemen on Eilean Mor.

There has been habitation in the Outer Hebrides for more than 5,000 years. Life in the islands was nearly always hard as people battled primarily against the elements to carve out an existence, and this continued up until the twentieth century. There is substantial evidence of the Iron Age past with Iron Age forts and archaeological sites scattered throughout the Isle of Lewis. The Vikings invaded the islands in the ninth century and left their mark, with many of the place names being of Norse origin. Perhaps the most outstanding example of the long history of the islands is the Callanish Stones,[1] which lay close to the village of Callanish on the west coast of Lewis. They were constructed between 2900 and 2600 BC, and it is believed that part of them may have been constructed earlier than 3000 BC. The thirteen primary stones form a circle roughly 40ft in diameter with a long approach avenue of stones to the north and shorter stone rows to the south, west and east. A tomb was later built into the site and excavations there in 1980 and 1981 discovered human remains and found evidence that the tomb had been added later as well as modified many times, and also that it had been out of use from 2000 BC and 1700 BC Looking from above, the whole site appears very roughly like a Celtic Cross. The main site is referred to as Callanish I as there are several other megalithic sites in the area and these are numbered accordingly. For example, Cnoc Dubh, an ancient settlement or 'Shieling' (a stone dwelling used while tending cattle on summer pastures,) is known as Callanish VII. The other sites, which are mainly stone settings or standing stones, are also named Callanish, with roman numerals to differentiate each one. In respect of the Callanish Stones, the folklore has a couple of variations. One of the local traditions states that the giants who lived on Lewis refused to be converted to Christianity by Saint Kieran, an Irish Monk, and were therefore turned into stone as a punishment. Another legend states that at sunrise on midsummer morning, a deity known as the 'Shining One' walks along the stone avenue, its arrival heralded 'by the Cuckoo's call'. The origin of this particular legend probably has its roots in some memory of the astronomical significance of the stones. Local folklore also relates the history of a race of 'small people' who were described as pigmies.[2]

A native of Lewis named John Morison made the first written references to the stones in around 1680. He wrote, 'great stones standing up in ranks ... were sett up in place for devotione.'[3] The religious significance of the stones was apparent from the earliest observations after they had fallen into disuse.

Although the islands have been uninhabited for the most part through the centuries, there have been two previous habitations (besides the lighthouse keepers) on Eilean Mor. The first were the religious men (St Flannan and associated monks who sought the island for spiritual retreat), from where the sanctity of the islands gained their reputation and much later, sheep were often taken to graze out on Eilean Mor with their attendant shepherds; although this would be for relatively short periods rather than extended stays on the island.

The main island of the group of seven largest rocks, Eilean Mor covers an area of 40 acres and at its highest point is 285ft. The Flannan Isles (Scottish Gaelic: Na-h-Eileanan Flannach) are known as the Seven Hunters. The islands are named after the seventh-century Irish preacher and Abbot, St Flannan. They were possibly known during the middle ages as the Seven Holy Isles. Despite being only just under 20 miles west of the Isle of Lewis, the islands are as lonely and isolated as can be found anywhere as they border the vastness of the North Atlantic.

The islands are split into three groups. There are two main islands: Eilean Mor (meaning Big Isle) and Eilean Taighe (meaning House Isle) and these lie to the north-east of the group. The main western islands (smaller than Eilean Mor) are Eilean a Gobha (meaning Isle of the Blacksmith), Roaireim and Brona Cleit (meaning Sad Sunk Rock). Lying to the south are the islands, or outcrops of rock, which perhaps would be a better description, of Soray (meaning Eastward Isle) and Sgeir Tomain. Roaireim is slightly different to the other islands by virtue of having a natural rock arch. There is a small ruined stone chapel on Eilean Mor and two stone structures, plus on Eilean Taighe there is a ruined stone shelter. All of these ruins are described by the Royal Commission of the Ancient and Historical Monuments of Scotland (RCAHMS) as 'The Bothies of the Clan MacPhail' or 'Bothain Chlann 'Ic Phail.' The origins of the name of Flannan are uncertain. It might refer to the seventh-century Abbot of Killaloe in County Clare, or to the half-brother of the eighth-century St Ronan, for whom the nearby island of North St Rona is named. The name could also originate from the son (named Flann) of an Abbot of Iona (named Maol-duine),[4] who lived until AD 890. In pre-history the area was covered in ice sheets spreading from Scotland westwards out into the Atlantic Ocean. When the ice sheets had receded about 20,000 BP[5], sea levels were around 400ft lower than the present day and it is likely that the islands were part of a larger land mass but still separated from the Outer Hebrides by open water.

People from Lewis would travel out to graze their sheep on Eilean Mor as well as raid the nests of the seabirds for eggs, birds and feathers. The abundance of birds included populations of northern fulmars, European storm petrels, Leach's petrels, black-legged kittiwakes, common shag and Atlantic puffins. It was and still is an ornithologist's delight, particularly the gannetry on the islands. And in the short history of any humans populating the islands, it was the lightkeepers who had introduced rabbits to the islands.

As one approaches the islands from Lewis and views them with numerous types of seabirds flying around them, it is tempting to cast your mind back to 15 December 1900 and try to imagine what happened to the three lightkeepers on the main island of Eilean Mor all those years ago. The islands are unchanged as you look at them from the sea. The only addition, the helicopter landing pad, cannot be seen from sea level; otherwise everything is exactly as it was on that day. The weather that day was not good with heavy seas and rain. The meteorological records for December 1900 showed the largest amount of monthly rainfall ever to have fallen that month in the locality and this record still stands at the end of 2013.[6]

The township of Breasclete (also referred to as Breascleit) would be considered small in most places, but in Lewis terms it was a fairly large settlement. It played an important role for the light station on the Flannan Isles as it was here (rather than at Stromness) that David Alan Stevenson chose to build the shore station for the lighthousemen and their families. Breasclete in the latter half of the nineteenth century contained over forty crofter families. It was also the site of a major investment, a fish processing plant, by the old Highlands and Islands Development Board. There were also associated facilities such as wharves and landing facilities built on Loch Roag. Unfortunately the venture failed, along with a further commercial venture, a fish oil company which sold oil capsules under the trade name of Callanish.

The automation of the Flannan Isles Lighthouse on 28 September 1971 also brought to an end the presence of personnel and families associated with the station on Lewis. Tourism fortunately still thrives in the Outer Hebrides, with the Flannan Isles serving as an attraction for day trips.

Notes
1 See British Geological Survey website for useful background: www.bgs.ac.uk.
2 See Chapter 8.
3 From his account of the Western Isles in 1680.
4 Wikipedia: en.wikipedia.org/flannan-isles. See also Clare Library: www.clarelibrary.ie for more information on St Flannan.
5 See British Geological Survey website for useful background: www.bgs.ac.uk.
6 See Appendix III for more weather details.

THE NLB AND THE LIFE OF A LIGHTHOUSEMAN

The seas around Scotland and the Scottish coastline itself have never been a place for the faint-hearted mariner. On the north-western side, the coast faces the full force of the North Atlantic winds and storms, although the islands of the Outer Hebrides act as a breakwater to the mainland. Off the eastern coast, the North Sea gives rise to frequent mists and fog such as the *Haar*[1], which often can appear very quickly and affects shipping and aircraft down on the lower eastern coasts of Scotland and northern England.

Prior to the full establishment of a system of lighthouses in Scotland, the appalling number of shipwrecks and loss of life around the wilder parts of the Scottish coastline left both seamen and those engaged in commercial trading to push for something to be done, as the number of wrecks around the Scottish coastline ran into thousands upon thousands and stood as a testament to the dangers faced by men who made their living from the sea. The roll call of shipwrecks ran from the earliest fishing vessels up to and beyond the oil tanker *Braer*, stranding in the Shetlands in 1993.

However, whilst there was no unnecessary unwillingness on the part of the government or local authorities to ease the plight of seafarers plying treacherous waters, everything, as always, came down to money; who was going to pay for it?

The actual building or placing of lighthouse stations around Scotland's coast was a long and laborious affair, although compared to the establishment of a system of lighthouses in England, it was completed in a shorter timescale, with the majority of the work being finished within a century.

The earliest lighthouse in Scotland was built on the Isle of May by James Maxwell of Innerwick and John Cunninghame of Barnes, under a patent granted by Charles I in 1635. The Isle of May lighthouse was bought from its then owners in 1814 and the present lighthouse was built and illuminated from 1816.

The origins of the NLB go back to 1782 after a series of severe storms brought home the lack of a proper lighthouse system around the coast of Scotland. The Commissioners of Northern Lighthouses, as it was initally known, was created in 1786 following an Act of Parliament, which allowed them to have the powers to purchase land, borrow money and levy dues from ships to finance their work and building. Initially the Commissioners were allowed to build four lighthouses, including Kinnaird Head in Fraserburgh.[2] A further impetus was given by two further Acts of Parliament in 1788 and 1789.

The Scottish local lights (which were much smaller than lighthouses) and seamarks had been constructed under local Acts of Parliament or Burgh Charters. Buddon Ness on the Tay was the earliest recorded light, constructed by an Act of the Privy Council in 1687. An Act in 1836 made these local lights and seamarks subject to the supervision and inspection of the Commissioners of Northern Lighthouses.[3]

The division of lighthouse responsibility in the British Isles eventually settled: Trinity House covered England and the Channel Islands (also including Europa Point Lighthouse at Gibraltar); Irish Lights, with headquarters in Dublin, covered both Eire and Northern Ireland; and the Northern Lighthouse Board covered Scotland and the Isle of Man. The exception to the system of Scottish lighthouses was the six lighthouses on the River Clyde, which had been owned and administered by two separate trusts before being amalgamated into the Clydeport Trust in 1966.

The story of lighthouses and their development in Scotland is strongly linked to one remarkable family. The best known member of that family is Robert Louis Stevenson, who is remembered for his outstanding writing. But it is the other members of his family who, though perhaps not as well known, are primarily responsible for the establishment of the network of lighthouses around the most dangerous parts of the Scottish coast.

Starting with the head of the line, Thomas Smith, there descended from him a procession of very capable and highly intelligent men who were fine examples of the Scottish talent for civil engineering.

Thomas Smith had married Jean Stevenson in 1787 taking on her son Robert as a stepson. It was her second marriage and his third. They were widow and widower and it was as much a marriage of convenience as attraction, as both had young children.

Although Thomas Smith was the head of the line as far as the actual connection with lighthouses goes (he was engineer to the NLB), the first of the actual Stevenson dynasty would be Robert Stevenson. In 1786, Robert Stevenson had put his studies to one side to learn the craft of working with iron and lights from his stepfather Thomas Smith. Between the two of them they set out to improve the system of lighting by replacing the early and unreliable fire-type lights, firstly with oil and then with gas, and improving the oil light system. The key to their progress was in the development of the use of optics. Notwithstanding their passion to improve the system of lighthouses in Scotland, they also immersed themselves in many other projects, most of which might be said to have the underlying theme, not just of engineering projects for their own sake to build or improve what was there, but to work for the greater good of mankind in general, and Scotland in particular. It was an embodiment of the Victorian principle of work being done in God's name for the benefit of all and not self-aggrandisement.

As civil engineers, inventors and designers, the works of the Stevensons extended far beyond lighthouses. Robert's three sons Alan, David and Thomas would follow in their father's footsteps and also become engineers. Alan Stevenson became a commissioner of the NLB, and when he retired his position was taken by his brother David.

Despite the self-imposed mission of each succeeding generation of the Stevenson men to pursue the goal of the improvement of the Scottish lighthouse system (along with numerous other civil projects), the Stevenson that really stands out was not known for civil engineering work or lighthouses. Robert Louis Stevenson was pushed by his father to continue the family dynasty and follow the tradition of becoming an engineer to the NLB. Despite being strongly pushed by his father, Thomas, he appears to have been temperamentally unsuited to the life and profession. Despite an attempt at pleasing his father by getting involved in the day-to-day work of civil engineering, his real love was literature, much to his father's annoyance. Nevertheless Robert Louis was able to use some of the experiences he gained during his time as an engineering apprentice in the wilder parts of the Scottish coast and to feature them in his novels. After a brief fling with studying law, which had the half-hearted approval of his father, Robert Louis eventually gave up all other pursuits and concentrated on his writing.

The particular skill that the Stevensons developed was in the construction of building a lighthouse, in many cases on nothing more than an outcrop of rock, far out to sea, with the hindrance of terrible weather including violent seas and high winds. All this would be done without the modern aids for building in the twentieth and twenty-first centuries. The haulage of the stone needed was another feat which required ingenuity. In particular, the building of the lighthouse on the Flannan Islands required considerable planning and the laying down of tram lines; moreover, the construction of steps into the cliffs for access to the site was necessary before building could even begin.

In addition to the building of lighthouses, Thomas Stevenson, with his brother David, put a considerable amount of effort into developing lighthouse optics using electricity. David had two sons, Charles and David Alan. Whilst they both continued with the family tradition of service to the NLB, much of the pioneering work had already been completed before them. However, David Alan was responsible for the building of the Flannan Isles Lighthouse, which in itself was no mean feat, along with the shore station at Breasclete.

David Alan Stevenson had first visited the Flannan Islands in 1893 to examine the location as to its suitability for a lighthouse station. His view was that the Isles lay dangerously near the track of vessels bound from the westward and making land and were taking the 'north about' passage which was used by a large number of ships.[4] He went on to describe the location as being 20 miles from Gallan Head (on the Isle of Lewis) and 46 miles north-north-east from Monach Lighthouse and was in the centre of a stretch of unlighted coast 75 miles in length between the Butt of Lewis and Monach. David Alan described the necessity for a light thus: 'Valuable assistance a light would afford to the increasing Atlantic trade passing near when passing westward, they grant their statutory sanction to the establishment of a lighthouse on these islands.'[5]

The main island of the group, Eilean Mor, was decided upon as being the most suitable, as apart from having a relatively flat and largely grassed area on top of the island, there was plenty of space and it was well elevated from the waterline – up to 150ft at many points and in some places higher. Initially Stevenson had wanted to place the light on the most westerly island of the Flannan Islands group, but it was not high enough to 'show the light over the others'. In addition, the most westerly island was even more difficult to land on and more inaccessible than the main island of Eilean Mor. In his report, Stevenson mentions that Eilean Mor rises to 280ft above sea level and that, of its 40 acres, 16 acres was grass-covered with the rest of it being rocks and cliffs along with the uninhabited 'Blessing Chapel'. He then mentions the two summits of the island being almost the same height and all around surrounded by practically vertical cliffs, none of which were less than 150ft. Stevenson had made his landing on the south side, as he called it, and recommended this as the best site to make an entry onto Eilean Mor. What he probably meant was the area of the west landing, which is on the south side of the island but turns so that it is facing westwards.

In an almost prescient comment about the tragedy which followed seven years later, Stevenson wrote: 'The landing of materials will obviously be attended with considerable difficulty for there is little protection from the Atlantic swell which is seldom at rest.'[6]

The major problem, however, was reaching this relatively flat grassy area, especially with all the building materials that would be required.

The site had been suggested as suitable for the placing of a lighthouse as early as 1853 by the Commissioners of Northern Lighthouses to the Board of Trade.[7] Nothing was done, however, and the matter lay for twenty-seven years when it was again brought before the Board of Trade by the Commissioners of Northern Lighthouses in 1880. Once more, the matter received a lukewarm response. Finally, in 1892, the elder brethren declined to give their sanction for the building of a lighthouse on Eilean Mor, but the Northern Lighthouse Commissioners appealed to the Board of Trade as arbiter and the board found in favour of the Commissioners. So after a near forty-year wait from when it was first suggested, the go-ahead was finally given for the Eilean Mor Lighthouse to be built. In his capacity as engineer to the Commissioners of Northern Lighthouses, David Alan Stevenson had again visited the Flannan Islands and looked at the various difficulties associated with the building of a lighthouse on Eilean Mor.

Stevenson had actually written two reports on the possibilities of a lighthouse on the Flannan Islands. The first was dated 3 January 1893.[8] The second report was dated 21 October 1895[9] and was duly presented to the Commissioners of Northern Lighthouses for their consideration.

In his report dated 3 January 1893, Stevenson broke down the building costs as follows:

Tower and Buildings on Eilean Mor:

As if built on shore	£1,600
Boundary walls and fencing	£200
Landing places, stairs and tramways	£1,625
Paths from south landing place	£60
Cranes, hauling engines etc.	£370
Temporary barracks, stores etc.	£310
Maintenance of workmen for 3 Seasons	£945
Shipping 3 Seasons, moorings and landing boats	£7200
Parapet, lantern, optical apparatus, revolving machine, lamps and fountains, and oil cisterns	£7,050
Dwelling houses for 4 lighthouse keepers at Stromness	£2,425
Land	£200

David Alan Stevenson stated in the report that his view was that if the work could be completed in two seasons instead of three, then the total amount would be reduced by about £2,000. The crux of the whole project was the light itself; he estimated the centre of the optical apparatus would be 328ft above sea level and would give a clear weather range of light of 24 miles. He also proposed that the Flannan light should give two flashes in quick succession every half minute.

Stevenson then turned his attention to the question of shore accommodation for the lightkeepers and their families. Initially he favoured Stromness. This, he stated, was due to the fact that the relief vessel (the lighthouse tender) *Pole Star* was stationed there. The alternative to building the cottages at Stromness was the nearest suitable location to the Flannan Islands, which was West Loch Roag and the small settlements at Breasclete and Carloway. The intention of building the lightkeepers' cottages at Stromness was so that, as the reliefs for the Sule Skerry Lighthouse Station were already made from there, it would be easier to also make the reliefs for the Flannan Islands from the same location. Stevenson estimated that doing both the Sule Skerry relief and the Flannans would only occupy the *Pole Star* for thirty hours in favourable weather. With this in mind he had surveyed three sites for the Flannan lightkeepers' cottages at Stromness.[10]

Despite his earlier preference for the establishment of the lighthouse keepers' shore accommodation to be at Stromness, Stevenson went on to write that Breasclete, with its good anchorage, would probably offer the most advantage in serving the Flannans.

On 9 February 1899 Stevenson wrote a letter[11] to the board of the Commissioners of Northern Lighthouses in which he gave the details of four quotations for hauling appliances to be used on Eilean Mor. He recommended Carrick & Sons as being the lowest. The four tenders were as follows:

Carrick & Sons	£242
Chaplin & Company, Glasgow	£378
West End Engineering Works, Edinburgh	£268
Messrs MacLellan, Glasgow	£270

Additionally, a specification[12] for an invitation to tender was given, dated 22 August 1899, for the furnishing and fittings including communication bells between the lightroom and living room. Bells were also provided between the bedrooms and the living room (the bells were 3' and 4' respectively). Stevenson involved himself in the minutest of detail, for example, specifying that the bells in the bedrooms were to be mounted on varnished pitch pine with the word 'Lightroom' to be engraved on them and the lightroom was to have boards of varnished pitch pine with the words 'Principal', '1st Assistant' and '2nd Assistant' engraved on each one. Even when it came to the wiring, which may have been expected to be left to an assistant to stipulate, Stevenson specified the type of wiring required and that it was to be tapered and tarred. He then described where the wire was to be laid, when it was to be placed in tin tubes and when it was to be left exposed. Contractors could submit a sample of the wire they proposed to use along with their tenders for the work. The specification also stated that the length of wire required could be obtained from the NLB headquarters at 84 George Street, Edinburgh. After then stating the requirements for batteries and spare parts, Stevenson finished with the prices and wages stipulations and the proviso that he expected all of it to be tried and properly tested and to be of the very best quality and finished to the entire satisfaction of the engineer (i.e. David Alan Stevenson himself) within one month from the date of acceptance of the offer. It is an exacting document and one that his grandfather would have been proud of. The Stevenson mania for hard work and the constant desire to plan and control the smallest detail of the work had passed down through the generations.

On the subject of the building work itself, Stevenson stated[13] that the total area to be used for buildings, paths and tramways came to 43,950sq. ft or 1.0009 acres. In setting out his proposals for the layout, Stevenson said that certain rights would have to be insisted upon. These included the right to quarry stone from any part of the island and the right to use any part of the island (Eilean Mor) for temporary buildings, stores, etc.

In 1900, only nine days prior to the disappearance of the three lightkeepers, Stevenson had made notes[14] on 6 December regarding discussions he had held with Lloyds and a proposed agreement for the installation of a wireless telegraph. The intention was for Lloyds to supply and erect the whole plant including instrument poles, a flag staff, flags and everything necessary for signalling purposes.

Of various other matters relating to the work on the lighthouse, two of note stand out. The first was the sudden death of the Clerk of Works, Mr Deas, who died at the end of the third season's work and the second was that principal contractor, Mr Lawson[15] was deeply unhappy at the cost overruns on the work, which he felt were through no fault of his own. Although the lighthouse was first to be officially lit in December 1899 and operated thereafter, the actual work carried out by Mr Lawson and his men did not officially finish until October 1900.

The lighthouse on Eilean Mor became operational on 7 December 1899 with a permanent roster of four keepers. The life of a lightkeeper was certainly different to any other profession, with its overtones of ranks, maritime associations and elements of civil service governance. It was also a job that was a way of life, as the lightkeepers were tied very closely to their place of work.

A grasp of the NLB rank structure is useful in understanding how the keepers related to each other. Each lighthouse was the responsibility of the principal lightkeeper (PLK). Under him, at lighthouses with a foghorn, he would have had two assistant lightkeepers (ALK). The general adoption of the forty-hour week in the UK by the early 1970s led the NLB to introduce local assistant lightkeepers (LALK). For many years most stations had already had occasional lightkeepers (OLK), normally at least one. They tended to be mainly local residents trained in lightroom duties and capable of standing a watch in an emergency or covering for holidays. It was by no means regular work, just as and when needed. It was decided to carry the concept of OLKs further, but a number of problems soon became apparent.

When they were built, mainland and island lighthouses were set up for three full-time career lightkeepers and their families, all living in cottages at the station which were provided free as part of their wages by the NLB. Two-man stations, and there were a few, were basically lighthouses without a foghorn or the impedimenta needed to operate one. At one point in the 1970s, there were a few one-man stations as well. These included Barns Ness, Buchan Ness, Cromarty and Chanory. These were manned by a PLK only, who would put the light on and then quite legitimately go to his bed. Their intended use by the 1970s was for the worthy notion of them being a final posting for PLKs approaching their retirement. Some said, perhaps unkindly, that in practice they ended up being used as a repository for the arguably less worthy PLKs, a place to put them, in effect, where they couldn't cause any more bother!

A little known fact is that, certainly in the second part of the twentieth century, minor or automatic lights were regarded as less reliable than the manned lighthouses and light-dues charged on them were accordingly considerably less.

Being a career lightkeeper also meant that every few years, just like the military, he was subject to being posted to another lighthouse, with the consequent family upheaval. This state of affairs lasted until the 1970s (and the forty-hour week) when it was decided to make local assistants established keepers. This would give them a full-time job, but they would remain at 'their' lighthouse, resident in their own home. This would remove at a stroke one of the Board's biggest headaches, i.e. providing accommodation at the station for their full-time keepers. Broadly speaking, they would be full-time lightkeepers, but would remain in one location with personnel rising from three to four full-time keepers, with obvious adjustments to the watch-keeping rota to take this into account. OLKs would still be retained and utilised as and when needed. Many OLKs were given the opportunity to become LALKs and quite a few did take advantage of the opportunity, but in other cases the job was advertised locally.

On the offshore 'rock' lighthouses, they had hitherto been manned by four keepers: a PLK and two ALKs, with a third ALK ashore. The 'rock' keepers and their families lived in various towns around the Scottish and Manx coasts with the men going out to do several weeks' duty at their stations, the changeovers being effected by either a local retained boatman or one of the three lighthouse tenders then in use. The main shore stations were in Oban, Granton and Stromness and generally consisted of several 'four in a block' houses, one for each lighthouse. In Stromness for example, there was Sule Skerry, Copinsay, Pentland Skerries and Stroma. Elsewhere, the families of those on Sanda lived in Campbeltown and Pladda in Lamlash, on Arran. Girvan accommodated the Ailsa Craig crew, and Breasclete the Flannans, so, as can be seen, the keepers and their families were fairly widely scattered. It could be said that double-manning the rocks was how the NLB chose to really bring themselves into the twentieth century. Once double-manning was introduced, each rock took on a complement of six keepers; two complete crews of three; two PLKs and four ALKs, so that there was always one complete crew on the rock and one ashore. A rock keeper would carry out twenty-eight days of duty at the lighthouse, followed by twenty-eight days ashore, where he would be free to do whatever he wanted. Generally, holidays would be taken during the twenty-eight days ashore.

Cape Wrath became a 'rock' when it was eventually deemed too remote for the families to remain. Council houses were provided in Dingwall, a fair distance away, and the keepers initially travelled backwards and forwards by taxi.

The lack of accommodation continued to bedevil the NLB's efforts in respect of double-manning. Their solution was to approach every relevant local authority in Scotland and get them to agree to let them have an appropriate number of houses for these extra keepers. The Board would pay the rent, rates and later council tax, as all these were part of the keepers' wages. This arrangement worked well enough initially, but the various authorities insisted that the houses had to be in the names of the keepers, not the NLB. When the implications of this filtered through to the workforce, several left the job as they had secured their own tenancy of a council house.

As automation progressed, this particular problem tended to solve itself, as more of the Board's own houses at these stations fell empty and families were moved into them; thus the NLB was able to retain a measure of control over the keepers' housing.

On joining, a new employee was provided with a free house, uniform, basic items of furniture, a certain amount of domestic stores and a free coal allocation. All of this was considered part of their wages, which were not deemed excessive. In this respect, the terms under which lightkeepers were employed had not really changed all that much since the service was established. It was said by one lightkeeper that working for the Board, in many ways, was like a step back into the past.

The life of a lightkeeper was not for everybody. A person would join as a supernumerary (SLK) at which point they started on their journey around Scotland's edge, which could last, in some cases, for many months.

Rubh'Re was a training station and as such the station saw a fair number of SLK pass through. However, every now and again, one would disappear en route, when, having been given a travel advance by the NLB headquarters in Edinburgh, they had obviously decided the life wasn't for them, taken the money and gone home. It tended to make life a bit more difficult at times for the other lightkeepers, more so if the station was waiting for one to arrive to relieve another so they could go on leave.

An SLK would be placed initially at a station as an 'extra' man to learn the drill from the established crew there. Eventually, as an SLK, once the months of travelling – a few weeks here, a few weeks there – were completed, he would be appointed to a station as a regular full-time career lighthouse keeper. It could have been a rock, a mainland lighthouse, or an island.

Everyone mostly got along with each other, but not always. Authority didn't come from merit or qualifications, just how long a person had been in the job.

Each lighthouse, whatever its location, worked exactly the same watch-keeping system of four hours on watch, followed by eight hours off. The navigation light, as it was referred to, was always lit at dusk and extinguished at dawn. To this end, a framed chart hung in every lightroom, detailing these times day by day for the entire year. The chart was replaced by another when BST changed to GMT and vice versa. Depending on the latitude and longitude of each lighthouse, the times would vary, of course, the further north or south you were; it was as precise as that.

Even as late as 1974, more than a few lights were still run on paraffin, just like a giant Tilley lamp and the mechanism which operated them was mostly hand-wound as well, similar to clockwork. Basically, the light, whatever its source, was fixed inside a large series of lenses. These lenses rotated around the light, giving the station its identifying flash; some ran on roller bearings and some floated (literally) in a bath of mercury. The 'machines' ran at various speeds which differed from lighthouse to lighthouse, thus giving each its own 'identity', which was of course printed on the Admiralty charts carried by all shipping, thus enabling the mariner to fix his position. As a very rough rule of thumb, in Scotland one generally could count on a major or minor light being situated around the coast every 20 miles or so.

Each machine was set to rotate at a specific speed in order to generate its own flash, and the prime duty of each lightkeeper was to ensure that the light was exhibited at the proper time and that it maintained its proper identity. A large weight was suspended at the end of a chain, or a steel cable attached to the machine. Initially a keeper would set the lens in motion, after lifting the blinds on the astragels (the windows right at the top of the lighthouse). Then, if it was a paraffin light, the keeper pre-heated the mantle by lighting two wicks in a small container of methylated spirits, opened the valve and then ignited the vapour using a large taper. The flame was then adjusted and the light was in operation. In the lightroom, there were two containers, one of compressed air and one of paraffin. The appropriate valves would be opened to ensure a steady supply of fuel to the light and the pressure was kept going via an attached stirrup pump. It was important to make sure the methylated spirit wicks were extinguished and the machine was running at the correct speed after winding it fully. Then, depending on circumstances, the keeper would maintain their watch in the lightroom, as they were supposed to do, or go back down all the stairs again, which many of them did.

Some machines ran for thirty minutes before they had to be rewound, some ran for forty or forty-five minutes and some ran for an hour. They all varied. Rewinding brought the weight back to the top again and whilst this was being carried out it was geared to keep rotating.

The ultimate sin was to 'stand the light' or to allow it to exhibit a false character. Doing so meant instant dismissal with the loss of not just the job but your home as well. It was a sobering thought in the broadest sense, as drink was also the downfall of more than one lightkeeper from the time the role was created.

Maintaining the watches appears more complicated than it actually was. One man came on at 6 p.m. and was on duty until 10 p.m., putting the light on if such action fell between these times. He would then hand over to the second man, whose duty was from 10 p.m. until 2 a.m.. He in turn handed over to the third man, who had been on duty the previous day from 10 a.m. until 6 p.m. The third man came back on duty at 2 a.m. until 6 a.m., when he in turn handed over to the first man, who had done the 6 p.m. until 10 p.m. watch the previous night. Generally, depending on the time of year, he would be the one to put the light out at dawn. Of course there were variations to this system of watchkeeping but it gives a good idea of how a working day for the lightkeepers was broken up. On the rock stations there were three keepers, whereas on mainland and island stations, with the introduction of L/ALKs, there were four. This had the bonus of letting them have a day or so off in rotation. When on a rock, a keeper did twenty-eight days' duty straight. Back on mainland or island stations one man was on duty all day, from 10 p.m. until 6 p.m., and he would be the one who came back on duty at 2 a.m.

At family stations, watches were usually, but not always, changed in 'the bothy', almost invariably a small, self-contained facility with a bunk, toilet, cooker etc. which would normally be used by the L/ALK and the OLK.

A good example of one procedure which had not changed since 1900 to the early 1970s was the system of calling bells, the name boards, which exact specifications David Alan Stevenson had assiduously described above. They were placed in such a position in the bedroom that the lightkeeper had to get out of bed to answer them, therefore achieving their purpose. Unless the wife of a lightkeeper was a particularly heavy sleeper, she would invariably also be awakened at the change of watch. Some wives eventually became so used to the bells, that the sound never bothered them. Some lightkeepers have said that it was hard to escape the feeling that they were merely the latest, and possibly the last, in a long line of lightkeepers to answer that bell.

Monthly Returns were considered to be the bane of an ALK's existence at some stations. They were generally repetitive and some felt they were totally unnecessary, particularly having to copy out all the lighting and extinguishing times each month. One lightkeeper would tell the story of his time on Stroma to illustrate this point:

> The returns had been made up and put in an envelope, ready to give to the boatman to put in the post to HQ in Edinburgh. Relief day came and as it was raining, he stuck the envelope under the cushion on the seat of the tractor to keep it dry and off he went. The relief took place and life went on. Several months later, he happened to lift the cushion and there was the envelope. He had forgotten to give it to the boatman. However in the intervening period no one

had enquired as to where they were, or why for that month, Stroma had not submitted any returns. That was the point at which he started to wonder if anyone ever looked at them. He had a vision of a huge room at the NLB headquarters at 84 George Street, Edinburgh stacked from floor to ceiling with envelopes containing returns from all over the country, which were never opened.

Each weekday morning, the PLK and usually one ALK (though sometimes the L/ALK would also attend as well) would gather together in the engine room to be advised by the PLK what the morning's tasks would be, whether cleaning or painting or whatever other tasks needed to be carried out. The 2 a.m.– 6 a.m. watch was generally excused as he would probably be asleep. This work detail only lasted until lunchtime, to give them the opportunity to get some sleep, as the keepers would all be keeping watch later.

Heating and cooking was usually via a coal-fired range, with possibly one or two paraffin heaters for domestic use. A kettle would always have been on the range. The existence and use of coal-fired ranges lasted at some stations into the 1960s. Fresh water would have been landed and stored in barrels. In addition to this, there was in many stations, some sort of catchment system for utilising rainwater for washing and toilet purposes. Usually, such water would be run off the roof into a stone cistern.

Weather observations were initially very basic, most likely limited to what could be seen with what was known as the Mk.1 'eyeball' from the station. Every tower usually had an outside temperature thermometer mounted on one of the astragels with its reading recorded daily. Again, in the earlier days, there was not a formal requirement for any other readings, nor indeed would any other meteorological instruments have been supplied. In later years certain stations were designated weather reporting sites and had various other instruments with which to carry out this task. These readings eventually found their way to the Meteorological Office at Bracknell, where they were incorporated into the Shipping Forecast.

On the Flannans, as at all the other rocks, one of the ALKs or OLKs would be designated cook for the week, switching over with his companion; the PLK being excused this task. With regard to provisioning in Scotland, it was felt that things were on a much more civilised level. The NLB was unlike Trinity House, where provisioning was carried out on a 'pooled' basis with one cook. With Trinity House, everybody basically did their own 'thing', i.e. obtaining and cooking their own food.

In the morning, after extinguishing the light and pulling the curtains over, whoever had the morning watch would have made all preparations for lighting-up that night. Brief details of the night's activities would have been recorded with pen and paper (originally this was on a slate), ready to be transferred to the log book by the PLK in due course. After breakfast, the other two would carry out any cleaning, maintenance or repair work on a daily basis, as well as whatever painting might be deemed necessary. This also kept them out of the cook's way. Everyone, including the cook, had to be mindful of upcoming watchkeeping duties and getting sufficient rest beforehand. Usually the lightkeeper who covered the 6 p.m.–10 p.m. shift would try to get his head down in the afternoon.

The NLB superintendent usually visited once a year, at which time he and the PLK would decide on what painting and other work had to be carried out at the station. This was paid work, fixed at a certain rate per hour and shared between all of them at the station. Generally, but not always, it involved painting. As previously mentioned, some stations undertook weather reporting for the Meteorological Office and this too was paid work, the Board charged the Meteorological Office heavily for their services. It was not compulsory, however, and some refused to do it even though the keepers were paid for their work. Where keepers on a station refused the work, this resulted in the task being given to the next lighthouse up or down the coast.

Another break to the monotony of the daily routine was the arrival of visitors. Anyone could ask to be shown around, provided it did not interfere with work. Mostly visitors were taken up the tower of a station in the afternoon. Among such visitors were politician and religious leader Ian Paisley and his family, who were shown around the Butt of Lewis on one occasion.

In the late nineteenth and early part of the twentieth century, the lightkeepers' diet was, broadly speaking, somewhat dull and stodgy. It consisted largely of bulk staples: dried peas, lentils, flour, potatoes etc. Any meat was usually salted to preserve it, mainly beef. There was also corned beef. There was always plenty of tea, of course, plus sugar in bulk, along with condensed and powdered milk. After a relief visit there may have been small amounts of fresh fruit and vegetables, although prior to electricity there were always preservation difficulties. Also after a relief there would perhaps be enough bread for the following few days. Some rock stations (although not the Flannans), had the luxury of having well-established vegetable gardens. On the more remote stations, there would be eggs available for short periods and, again after a relief, possibly a side of bacon, and oatcakes would be eaten once the bread had run out. The constant difficulty would have been food preservation; however, one staple that was always available to the lightkeepers in bulk was porridge.

Prior to the use of helicopters for carrying out reliefs, each station would have had a store of emergency rations, which would mainly consist of a variety of tinned foodstuffs, only to be utilised in the event of a relief going overdue. This happened on a fairly regular basis in those days, when rock reliefs were mostly carried out by the tenders. The emergency stock was dated and the lightkeepers would regularly rotate the tins. A visit to the Flannan Isles lighthouse by a Church of Scotland minister in April 1900 records a meal shared with the lightkeepers (William Ross and James Ducat are recorded as being present, as Ducat asked the minister to say a blessing for the meal and William Ross had prepared and cooked the food). The minister described the meal as plain fare but abundant with broth, beef and excellently cooked mashed potatoes followed by plum pudding.[16]

It can be said that the life was a singular one in all respects. At mainland or island lighthouses, where the families lived, whether they liked it or not, it was inevitable that they were part of the job too. At mainland stations, a semblance of family life could be maintained for all three keepers, and the keepers' children went to school locally. One such example was in Wester Ross. This was a very remote mainland station, so much so in fact that it was provided with its own station car (an Austin 1100), which the keepers took turns to drive.

This lighthouse was not regarded as a schooling station due to its distance from Gairloch (the nearest village), and one keeper there was transferred to the Butt of Lewis when his child reached school age.

This closeness to one another could, and did at times, lead to strained relations among the keepers. The keepers generally got along with each other, although the nature of the work demanded that they do so. There were exceptions to this but it can be said that people generally would find their own level and attempt to fit in somehow. Living in such close proximity developed an atmosphere of mutual tolerance that would certainly not have been the case in other situations. It was a unique existence, one which may very well have held everyone together. Despite this close proximity, more than one keeper stated that they would not describe another keeper as a friend. They were there not by choice, but because the Board had dictated that they serve there. Generally, they tended to respect each other's privacy and simply got on with it, though this was obviously difficult at times. This description of keepers and their families finding accommodation together was certainly not new and went right back to the beginning of the service.

The essential element in the make-up of a keeper was self-discipline, as without it they could not have functioned as a unit. It has been said by some keepers that a number of PLKs failed to recognise this and tended to take themselves far too seriously, forgetting that they were there only by virtue of their length of service and nothing more. All keepers were perfectly capable of carrying out the tasks of a PLK and indeed many of them did so when a PLK took leave or suffered periods of illness. A number of keepers felt that this facet of their inter-relationship with PLKs was often overlooked.

It cannot be denied that on the rock lighthouses, life for the keepers could be difficult at times and everything would depend very much on the personalities of the other two whom a keeper would be 'on' with; keepers were there for twenty-eight days straight, day and night, in close proximity to each other and it could, and did, get 'tricky'.

The ALKs took it in turns to cook the three meals a day, the PLK being exempt from this 'onerous' burden, which upset some ALKs, but most simply got on with it. The cook was, at least, exempt from day work (such as painting and cleaning) for the duration of his time in the kitchen.

As far as meals went, individual tastes were generally not catered for. This led to some amusing episodes, such as one which occurred on a station where 'mince and tatties' was a firm favourite. On one particular day the ALK, who was duty cook, noticed that the recently arrived PLK had picked all the carrots out of his portion, announcing his distaste for them. The next time 'mince and tatties' were served, the ALK had chopped up the carrots even smaller, but again the PLK repeated his performance of taking all the carrots out. Finally, for the next occasion, the ALK grated all the carrots, at which point the PLK gave up in disgust.

Overall, relations were good, but as with any organisation there would inevitably be the occasional management and worker disputes. One keeper's view was that, over the years, it had been the NLB's unofficial response to give 'awkward' fellows a 'bad' posting sooner or later; nothing could be proved of course, but his perception was that their patience was infinite and their memory of 'past misdeeds' long. Some PLKs had reputations of being particularly difficult on one rock. In one instance, a situation reached the stage where the ALKs refused to board the helicopter with one such individual. But luckily the virtual mutiny was avoided by leaving the PLK ashore. Eventually a suitable posting was found for the PLK and everything settled down. It was also believed by some keepers that if someone looked like actually achieving something advantageous for the workforce, he would then be promoted into management. One PLK was eminently successful in setting up a union for lightkeepers and he eventually became Depot Manager at Oban, a job that had hitherto been closed to keepers. He was the only one of the keepers ever to rise to this level, with his predecessors and successors usually being appointed from the Tenders. Another who made substantial progress as one of two Union representatives was offered, and subsequently accepted, the newly created post of Welfare Officer, based at 84 George Street, Edinburgh. He was considered to be, and eventually proved to have been, an excellent choice.

It would be perfectly correct to say that in essence, the work carried out by James Ducat, Thomas Marshall and Donald Macarthur in 1900 would not have been greatly different to the work carried out by lightkeepers seventy-odd years later. Automation had started in the 1960s and some, but by no means all, lights had been electrified. The technology which is taken for granted in the twenty-first century simply did not exist in 1900. From the 1900s, there would also have been some changes to creature comforts, and aids to the working of a lighthouse, such as the advent of radio and foghorns.

The introduction of foghorns benefited seamen but brought other problems for the lighthousemen operating them. Sudden mist or fog was always a possibility and on one occasion at one station, the foghorn stayed on for a full week after the fog had descended. The sound at such close quarters made talking difficult, and there was an art to having a conversation and building it around the sounding of the horn. Also the sound of running generators for twenty-eight continuous days could be 'tuned out'. A keeper on Skerryvore said that he was so used to the sound of the generator that the silence, when he went on leave, nearly drove him mad.

Most foghorns were of the siren type. They were generally located in a small building of their own, situated close to the water's edge and some distance from the living accommodation. When originally built, the direction of some of the horns would have been able to have been adjusted, but over the years this was discontinued and the majority were fixed. To power the foghorn, there was an engine-room, three engines – generally but not always Kelvin diesels – along with their associated compressors. To run the horn, two out of the three were used, with the third being kept as a spare in case of 'failure to start'. The whole apparatus was a mass of pipes, wheels and valves. Once started, there would be two engines up and running, and the air in the large tanks outside would build up to its operating pressure. Then the final outside valve would be opened, allowing the air down the line to the horn-house, where it would start to spin the siren. There was a built-in timing device, like the navigation light, and each foghorn could be identified by its particular series of blasts.

The duty keeper always kept an eye on the visibility, as sometimes it could deteriorate very rapidly. There were distance markers, which were set in such a way that if the sight of them was lost, the foghorn would be started up without delay. Lightkeepers were adept at carrying on a conversation, pausing for each blast of the horn. There were no ear-defenders back then either, which would probably not be the case today if lighthouses were still manned. Fog charts which recorded the duration of the run, were retained and sent to headquarters at 84 George Street, along with the returns every month. Due note was taken of fuel and lubricating-oil consumption.

One of the biggest changes that set rock reliefs apart from 1900 to the latter part of the twentieth century was how they were carried out. Helicopters have been mentioned previously and it was their use that revolutionised lighthouse reliefs, which no longer depended on the weather, as was so often the case with tender or attending boat reliefs.

For example, every two weeks a Bolkow 105 helicopter operated by Bond Helicopters out of Peterhead would be used for reliefs. Two keepers came out with the 'main relief', and two would go ashore. All the supplies and personal effects were packed into plastic boxes that were specially designed to fit into the Bolkow's hold. The helicopter always carried an engineer who flew 'up front' with the pilot, the keepers behind them.

Occasionally someone would be fortunate enough to travel alone on a 'mid relief',[17] with one keeper who travelled on the basis that 'any fool can be uncomfortable', and usually took about twice as many boxes as the others, which inevitably caused some grumbling. Travelling solo at times had other advantages; for instance, the distance from Campbeltown to Sanda was fairly short, so now and again the pilot would leave the engineer on the Green at Campbeltown, from where they were picked up and deposited, and come out for the solo keeper on his own. Almost all of the pilots were ex-Army Air Corps, to whom 'nap of the earth' flying was second nature. Transporting the keepers around was usually a far more sedate affair, carried out at (for them) a relatively high altitude.

Prior to the use of helicopters for leave reliefs, helicopters had been used to deliver supplies and newspapers to some of the rock lighthouses on a very irregular basis. On 15 December 1955 there was, however, a tragedy involving one of the RAF Leuchars Search and Rescue helicopters. The helicopter was a Bristol Sycamore, serial no. XG501 of 275 Squadron, based at RAF Leuchars, and was attempting to carry out a winching exercise on the Bell Rock Lighthouse. However, on this particular day, something went tragically wrong. The blades hit the anemometer of the lighthouse and the helicopter plunged into the sea right alongside the tower. The lightkeepers were quick to react with Bob Wood, one of the ALKs and a strong swimmer, diving in off the entrance flat with a rope around his waist, supported by the other two lightkeepers. Sadly, his considerable bravery was to no avail, as the crew of two were dead. Bob Wood won the Queen's Commendation for Brave Conduct for his actions that day, which many felt was well deserved. The light itself had sustained considerable damage and remained extinguished for five days until the necessary materials were sent out for its repair. Bob Wood stayed in the job and rose to PLK before he eventually retired, a good and brave man. Even as late as the spring of 1974, there were still quite visible dents in the dome of the Bell Rock Tower, which served as a sobering reminder of a rescue exercise gone badly wrong. Despite an extensive sea and air search, the body of the pilot, Flight Sergeant P.A. Beart, was never found.

On a lighter note, there was another connection between RAF Leuchars and the Bell Rock. A lightkeeper who had served there found that one of the questions he was (surprisingly) most often asked was: 'Is there a toilet on the Bell Rock?'.

There was, of course, in the entrance flat – a seawater toilet which had to be refilled after usage. Another method was almost standard operating procedure for some and this was to take a suitable newspaper and head for the balcony. Upon the conclusion of one's business, the then rolled-up newspaper would be jettisoned into the North Sea. For many years, there hung in the SAR helicopter crew room at Leuchars, a framed photograph of a certain PLK (now deceased) trying to keep his newspaper in place with one hand, whilst shaking his fist at a hovering Leuchars helicopter with the other. The whereabouts of this picture are unknown since the helicopters moved to Lossiemouth.

Any difficulties with relationships between a PLK and ALKs tended to lie below the surface, although more overt displays of friction can be found in the NLB records of dismissals for assault, including one in the late 1800s for assault on a keeper's wife. In the main though, friction would manifest itself in more juvenile behaviour such as that shown to one new PLK at a station, who was considered by the ALKs to be a serious sort of fellow, totally devoid of any sense of humour. This led to schoolboy jokes being played: in one instance, as a result of the PLK's penchant for locking everything up during the day, including the light tower, the key was removed from the lock and hidden just before he was due to light. As lighting time got nearer and nearer the principal was getting more desperate but did not want to reveal what was troubling him. When he started to panic, the key would be found by the assistants.

Whilst it may seem surprising that such schoolboy pranks would be indulged in, they served as a safety valve and probably stopped a build-up of more serious interpersonal problems, which could result in dismissal of one or more parties. The pranks also extended to visitors. At least once a year a station would be visited by the Board's artificers (engineers), who would stay for approximately a week or so, overhauling the engines, generators and machinery. Usually there were three in the party, so catering for double the usual number could put something of a strain on the normally tranquil existence of a station. One year, after the visitors' extended use of the bathroom at one station, the keepers decided to do something about it. An old boiler suit was filled with cotton waste, so as to resemble a human figure, and early one morning, before the visitors arose, this was placed on the toilet in the bathroom, where its vague outline could be discerned 'in situ' through the frosted panes in the toilet door. The perpetrator had locked the door from the inside, exiting through the window. The next morning, when they arose, the first one headed off for his morning ablutions only to discover the room was occupied. Nature took its course and the artificers were far from amused but, as was stated by the keepers, such diversions kept them entertained. The dummy itself lasted beyond this caper. It was tidied up, given a cap and seated in a shady corner at the pier. One day, when the *Fingal* arrived to top up the fuel supply, the dummy was still in a secluded spot on the pier. The ship's launches brought in the fule in relays and pumped it into the station's storage tanks ashore. It was a process that usually required the assistance of all hands. So when the bosun of the *Fingal* saw this idle fellow sitting watching the rest of them hard at work, he let forth a string of swear words, some of which even the keepers hadn't heard before. Fortunately, the bosun later saw the funny side of things. As for the dummy, it was last seen swimming in the general direction of Rathlin Island on the other side of the North Channel.

Despite the great seriousness of 'standing the light', it could have its amusing aspects. One night, at an island light, an off-duty keeper was awakened from his sleep, although he did not know what had roused him. An elderly OLK was on duty at the time, and the off-duty keeper, on looking out of the window, could see that the light was quite plainly standing and illuminating a passing fishing boat in its stationary beam. He flew out of the door and up the tower; in the lightroom was the old boy fast asleep, his false teeth perched on the table beside him. He quickly rewound the machine, the noise of which would have wakened the dead, but the OLK slumbered on. Having completed the rewinding, the off-duty keeper decided that perhaps discretion might be the better part of valour and to say nothing about the incident, which is precisely what he did. Nothing was ever mentioned by anyone, not even the OLK, who woke up shortly thereafter and wondered why the off-duty keeper (staying to check the light was OK) was present.

More than one keeper, who has spent any length of time in service, has mentioned the development of an almost extra sense which they have found hard to explain, but in the tower of a lighthouse at night, one would get attuned to certain normal sounds, smells and what has been described as feelings, thus the presence of something other than those normal senses would be very apparent. An example of this 'extra sense' was from a lightkeeper who explained that although they were supposed to remain in the tower when on watch, in practice this rarely happened, particularly if there was something good on the television (this was pre-video recorder days). The PLK at one particular station was known to be in the habit of sometimes just standing in the tower on the catwalk by the lens and saying nothing when others were on watch and went up to wind, which was considered to be very bad form and 'just not done'. On one occasion the keeper went through the door into the tower and felt straight away that something was amiss. As he entered the lightroom he could see the feet of the PLK above him. Saying nothing, the keeper rewound the machine then headed back down to the door and grabbing the key as he left, he locked the door behind him and ran into his house, switched the lights off and stood at the kitchen window and waited. After ten minutes or so the PLK's wife appeared from their house and went up to the tower and unlocked the door to let the PLK out – unbeknown to all, they had a spare key. Aside from this 'sense' developed by keepers, these little tricks may seem foolish with the passing of the years, but at the time it was felt that they helped them pass the time, which otherwise could hang heavily in their isolated stations.

Another aspect of the isolation of lighthouses meant that the lightkeepers were not overly concerned about being troubled by any 'outsiders'. One night, on Sanda, a lightkeeper was getting undressed for bed and had not bothered to pull the curtains – there was no need, the lightkeepers being the only human inhabitants of the island. The night was pitch black and he casually looked out the window to see a face staring in at him. Apparently, his scream was something to hear. The face belonged to a member of a yacht crew whose vessel yacht had come to anchor for the night on the other side of the island. However, they had come right inside, past the pier, before dropping their anchor and settling down. Fortunately, the bottom of the bay was both flat and sandy, for at low water, the vessel found itself on its side, high and dry. The crew had walked ashore, hoping to find someone at the lighthouse. The duty man was up in the lightroom, the PLK was already asleep and the terrified lightkeeper, in his bedroom, had been the only light visible at ground level. It was a great shock to find anyone but themselves in these locations.

It is worth mentioning that the Isle of Man occupied a special position within the NLB stations. In the days of manned lighthouses, the Isle of Man was regarded as something of a plum posting for the keepers, due to the low tax regime there. Being independent of the UK, the Manx Government had the responsibility for lighting its own coastline. It may seem odd that the NLB, with its primary area of operations in Scotland, should also be responsible for the Isle of Man, located much further south in the middle of the Irish Sea. However it came within the jurisdiction of the NLB from 1815, with a further Act of Parliament in 1854 enabling lighthouses to be built there should they be required after the initial two stations were built. Despite the presence of the NLB in the Isle of Man, the areas of responsibility of Trinity House and Irish Lights run fairly close to the Manx coast, and one of Trinity House's buoys is actually located off the east side of the island. However, living on the Isle of Man did have its drawbacks for 'incomers' such as the keepers. Their residential status was somewhat ambivalent in that although the keeper was sent to do duty at whatever Manx lighthouse he was posted to, and his family naturally went with him, when it came to wives, sons or daughters working full-time that was considered to be a different matter entirely. In the summer high-season, the authorities were never unduly bothered about the status of workers. However in winter, any non-Manx workers were obliged to apply for a work permit in order to continue their employment. In practice, they were rarely granted to lightkeepers' dependents. Eventually, it was deemed unnecessary for a lightkeeper's dependents to have to obtain a work permit in order to continue all-year-round employment.

Some keepers have said it is still difficult for them to explain the sheer grinding routine, but each of them coped in their own way. Some were great readers. Others made models, some fished, some even knitted.

At Sule Skerry, in common with the other rocks, there was a supply of coffin boards (just in case). It was often said that 84 George Street had thought of everything. One resourceful keeper, who had previously been a boatbuilder by trade, built himself a small dinghy using the coffins, which was highly unofficial of course. He used it for fishing around the rock and eventually took it home via the *Pole Star* on one relief to Stromness, where it remained for many years thereafter.

Each lighthouse station had its own particular characteristics and a station favoured by one lightkeeper would not necessarily be favoured by another. For instance Dubh Artach is still considered by one retired lightkeeper to be a dark and sinister place. He related how, on one occasion in the 1970s, the coal fire in the kitchen/living room became out of control and accidentally set the place on fire. It was a close-run thing; it could have been dangerous, if not fatal, as the whole place was lined with tongue-and-groove wood panneling. Acting promptly, the lightkeepers managed to extinguish the fire fairly quickly and the end result was largely limited to smoke damage. However, the question was – what to do? If they officially reported it, there was a very real chance that they would all be dismissed. This was not a prospect that any of them relished so they collectively came up with a novel solution; they simply stripped off the wood, turned it around, refitted it and then gave everything a fresh coat of paint. The whole incident was only mentioned to a very few people and then nothing more was said. The status quo remained until automation when all the internal wood would have been stripped out of the tower. Nevertheless, it was felt to be a positive solution to a potentially very tricky problem.

Despite the fears of the 'firestarting' Dubh Artach lightkeepers, instant dismissal for what was basically an accident was not necessarily a forgone conclusion. In a similar case, on the NLB Chicken Rock Lighthouse off the south coast of the Isle of Man, almost the same type of accident occurred in 1960, but with far more serious consequences. Chicken Rock was a three-man rock lighthouse, and the keepers and their families were housed in Port St Mary. It was not unlike Skerryvore in appearance, although it was much smaller. The lighthouse had a coal fire in the kitchen in those days and one day a fire broke out that rapidly went out of control to such an extent that the lightkeepers were forced to abandon the tower. They spent a wet and miserable night on the rocks before being picked up by the local lifeboat, all thankfully unhurt. The tower itself was totally burnt out and when it was eventually rebuilt it was never remanned, becoming an early candidate for automation in 1961. The blame for the fiasco was laid squarely at the feet of the PLK who was reprimanded and 'reduced to the ranks' as an ALK. However, the burden of his guilt was not carried forever, and in later years he became a PLK yet again – he is thought to be the only individual in the NLB to achieve this distinction. Whilst it is true that an accident is just that – an accident – and that the burning out of a lighthouse was not a deliberate act, in many ways the position of a PLK was similar to that of the captain of a ship in that the responsibility was ultimately theirs and that they were paid to accept the consequences of whatever went wrong under their command.

Despite the long hours and days of monotony experienced by the lightkeepers, especially on the tower and rock stations, both world wars brought an added strain to a number of lighthouses in Scotland.

An attack on a lighthouse may seem especially senseless but all the NLB lighthouses were still fully manned during both wars and came under strict Admiralty control. They were considered essential for shipping, particularly convoys. Accordingly, the lights would only be illuminated very briefly at specified times, usually to mark the passage of coastal convoys or single ship movements. All of them were 'blackened' i.e. hastily overpainted with a concoction of soot, usually from the station's own resources. After the Second World War the towers would be limewashed, and for many years afterwards large 'flakes' would occasionally break off so that the black wartime finish could still be discerned.

In the case of the Flannan Isles, the First World War came close to home with the sinking of two vessels by U-boats. The first sinking took place on 14 June 1915, when the Norwegian cargo ship SS *Davanger*, owned by Westfal-Larsen & Co A/S, Bergen, was on a voyage from Liverpool to Arkhangelsk. She was shelled and sunk by the German U-boat U-33, 12 miles west-south-west of the Flannan Isles. Over a year later, on 30 October 1916, the *Floreal* (a British fishing vessel of 163 tons) was sunk by U-boat U-57 approximately 20 miles north-west of the Flannan Islands.

During the Second World War, the lighthouses and their occupants, in the eyes of Luftwaffe crews, were providing assistance to the economic and military war effort of the Allies and despite being civilian-run, became quite legitimate targets for attack. There were twenty-four separate attacks by the Luftwaffe on lighthouses in the Second World War; the most seemingly senseless was on the South Fair Isle Lighthouse in December 1941 when the wife of an ALK was killed. In a second attack January 1942 the keepers' accommodation block was destroyed, killing the principal lightkeeper's wife, daughter and a soldier who was stationed nearby. A further attack in 1942 completely destroyed the accommodation block and it had to be rebuilt. Evidence of these attacks can still be seen in the form of pock marks on the tower itself and the outline of bomb craters just outside the lighthouse walls. Fair Isle South was the last lighthouse to be automated in Scotland on 31 March 1998. The accommodation block was sold to the National Trust for Scotland and eventually became bed and breakfast accommodation. Fair Isle had been designed by David Alan Stevenson and first lit in 1892, after which his next project was the new lighthouse on Eilean Mor.

Another example of a station attacked by the Luftwaffe was Rattray Head, located on the east coast of Scotland, north of Peterhead. Machine-gun damage to the lens was still apparent over thirty years later.

Rattray Head was regarded by more than one lightkeeper as a strange place. It was located maybe 500 yards or so along a very long, straight and sandy beach. It also had what was believed at the time (1970s) to be the longest unsupported length of telephone cable in the United Kingdom. The cable ran from the shore station, a short distance behind the sand dunes, where the four keepers were said to live in 'splendid isolation', to the tower. To the amusement of some and the annoyance of others, the cable was regularly carried away by very low-flying jets, mainly from the Royal Naval Air Station at Lossiemouth. What might be described as its only other claim to fame was that it was the only Scottish rock lighthouse where the relief was carried out by tractor. The tractor driver was officially referred to as the boatman and he also resided at the shore station with his 'trusty steed'. At least one tractor had been lost there when it was caught by the incoming tide, the remains of which could still be seen for some time afterwards some distance up the beach.

The lightkeepers on the rock, unofficially and at their own risk, could and did frequently walk ashore to their houses. There was nothing particularly wrong with this as long as they paid heed to the tide times in relation to when they were due to go on watch. There was a small rock, about halfway across, and so long as it could be seen it was considered safe enough to 'walk on'. The 'half-tide rock', as it was known, was an exceedingly important navigation aid in its own right. Mistakes did happen, of course, and this could lead to some nervous yet exciting times in their efforts to beat the tide, up to and including swimming for it. Rattray Head was said to run with damp and condensation, and with a large foghorn an integral part of the structure, sleep, at times, was certainly difficult.

More than one lightkeeper was glad to move on to another station at the end of his tenure.

The foregoing provides a general description of what the life of an NLB lightkeeper was like, and, other than technological improvements, life was unchanged in many ways from when Ducat, Marshall and Macarthur set foot on the Flannan Isles.

The life and work of an NLB lightkeeper can best be summed up as ordinary folk doing an extraordinary job.

Notes

1 *Haar.* As explained in the text, this fog only affects the east coast of Scotland, not the west coast
2 Information provided by NLB
3 None of these lighthouse organisations retain any manned lighthouses
4 Stevenson Archive National Library of Scotland File Acc.10706/119–123
5 Ibid
6 Ibid
7 Ibid
8 Ibid
9 Ibid
10 Ibid
11 Ibid
12 Ibid
13 Ibid
14 Ibid
15 Memo on costs from David Alan Stevenson, 8 January 1901, Scottish National Archives File No. NLC3/1/1
16 Account of visit by a minister to Flannan Isles Lighthouse, April 1900, in *Scotsman*, 29 December 1900
17 A 'mid relief' was one keeper out and one keeper in. A 'main relief' was two keepers out and two keepers in.

THE LIGHTKEEPERS AND A RECONSTRUCTION OF 15 DECEMBER 1900[1]

With the absence of the official log (as confirmed by the NLB headquarters at 84 George Street, Edinburgh), it can only be surmised as to what actually took place on the last day the lightkeepers were known to be present on Eilean Mor. However, a reasonable guess can be made of what happened up until the last entry on the slate.

The PLK was James Ducat. The son of a ploughman, he was born at Lunanbank Farm in the parish of Inverkeillor, near Arbroath on 11 August 1856 and he entered the service of the NLB as an ALK on 21 November 1878 at the age of twenty-two. In his position as an assistant, his first lighthouse was Montroseness (more commonly known as Scurdieness) where he spent seven months. He then moved to Inchkeith on 9 April 1879 where he stayed considerably longer, a total of five years and eight months. His lengthy period of service at Inchkeith was followed by an even longer period of service at his next lighthouse at Rhinns of Islay where he started on 3 March 1885 and spent a total of seven years and nine months. His almost eight-year span at Rhinns of Islay was followed by two shorter spells at Langness, for almost three and a half years. He received his promotion to PLK shortly after a move to Loch Ryan on 17 April 1896. His promotion to PLK was on 2 May 1896. On his arrival at Eilean Mor on 28 August 1899 James Ducat was therefore an experienced and seasoned lightkeeper with twenty-two years of experience behind him, including seniority as a PLK for over four and a half of those years.[2]

The Second ALK, and the third man in line of seniority on the Eilean Mor Lighthouse, was Thomas Marshall. He was born on 11 April 1871 and had entered the service of the NLB at the age of twenty-five as an ALK on 27 April 1896. His first station was Skerryvore where he arrived on 27 August 1896 and stayed three years and four months before his next posting to the Flannan Isles, arriving there on 31 August 1899. Marshall's NLB register entry also shows him to have been 'Seaman & Resident Occasional, Ailsa Craig'. No dates are given for Marshall's functions as seaman and OLK at Ailsa Craig, but it can be assumed that this was a period of training in the four plus months from when he joined the NLB in April 1896 to when he went to Skerryvore in August 1896. At the time of his disappearance on 15 December 1900, he was twenty-nine years old and had been an ALK for four years and nine months.[3]

On 15 December 1900, the third lightkeeper who should have been present on Eilean Mor was First Assistant Lightkeeper William Ross. However, he had been taken ill and been replaced by an OLK, Donald Macarthur. Macarthur was known to have a volatile temper and had only been in the service of the NLB for less than a year, having joined as an occasional on 29 January 1900 and undergone twenty-six nights' training since that date. So fate had led the unfortunate Macarthur to be present at the lighthouse on the 15 December when he should have been ashore at Breasclete on Lewis. Fate had, however, been kind to the fifth member of the full complement of staff, Third Assistant Lightkeeper Joseph Moore, whose turn it was to be on shore leave.[4] Due to a mix of fortunes, William Ross, who was described[5] as a powerfully built man, was lucky that he was not present on 15 December 1900. He had been unfortunate enough that injury and illness meant that he required medical attention away from Eilean Mor on two separate occasions in

1900. On the first occasion William Ross had been helping to unload provisions from the *Hesperus*. He had been sitting in one of the trolleys used to bring materials up to the lighthouse when the brake failed. Unable to jump off in time, Ross was forced to hang on as best he could, while the trolley gathered speed and went flying down the tramway to the east landing where it hit the buffers and he was catapulted into the air and landed on the rocks 15ft below, breaking his arm. He could quite easily have been killed and he was fortunate that the *Hesperus* was present and was able to take him back to the mainland immediately for treatment. The second time, Ross also escaped with his life, due to his absence because of illness on that fateful December day.

Occasional Lightkeeper Donald Macarthur, who had taken the place of William Ross, was a tailor by trade and had served in the Royal Engineers. He was well respected in Breasclete and was an upstanding member of the Free Presbyterian Church. Donald had been assisting in the construction of the Church at the time of his disappearance.

At 10 p.m. on Friday 14 December 1900 the watches changed and Donald Macarthur took over from the PLK, James Ducat. It was still not considered late but the conscientious and amiable Ducat would have been glad of the opportunity to go to his room and get some sleep. There were strong winds still blowing and a very heavy swell, which was the build up to an Atlantic storm. Once Macarthur was ready, the first thing he would have done would have been to go straight up to the lightroom on the relatively short tower and check that everything was in order and functioning properly. Thereafter, he would have spent an uneventful watch listening to the wind and the waves hitting the cliffs which surrounded Eilean Mor. He most likely would have alternated his time between the lantern room and the kitchen where he would have made himself tea from the ever-boiling kettle on the stove. Periodically, he would make sure he was in the lightroom to wind the mechanism back to its starting point to keep the light turning and giving out its flashes. While he was doing this, both Ducat and Marshall would be sleeping soundly in their beds catching up on their sleep, the lack of which was seemingly the bane of every lightkeeper's life when they were on their stations. After checking the lightroom one last time just prior to the end of his watch, Macarthur then went to Marshall's room to rouse the sleeping man and inform him that it was now Saturday and coming up to 2 a.m. and therefore time for his watch. No matter how many times a lightkeeper had done it, getting dragged out of bed on a wild winter's night was never enjoyable. Marshall would have swung himself out of bed and then stumbled over to the wash basin and washed himself before getting dressed and making his way to the kitchen for a cup of tea before going up to check on the lantern. Donald Macarthur was duty cook and decided to avail himself of four to five hours' sleep just after Marshall had gone to attend to the lantern. By 6 a.m. the weather was still fairly wild with high winds and large seas both approaching the Flannan Isles from a westerly direction. Marshall finished his watch and came down from the tower to rouse James Ducat who had completed the 6 p.m. to 10 p.m. shift the previous night, Friday 14 December. Despite the early start he was reasonably refreshed, having had nearly eight hours of sleep.

Although he had finished his watch, Macarthur, as mentioned, was also duty cook for the week and after sleeping for about five hours, he awoke to start preparing breakfast just after 7 a.m.. Breakfast was very much standard fare of plenty of tea, possibly boiled eggs, porridge and oatcakes. He would have brought water in from the tank where it was collected and stored, which was located just outside and along from the kitchen window.

At daybreak and after they had all eaten breakfast, Ducat would have extinguished the light, although it would be a grey gloomy morning with heavy overcast skies, and rain and spray carried by the strong westerly wind from the turbulent sea breaking on the rocks and cliffs around the island. Once the light had been extinguished, Ducat would have drawn the blinds and then set about refilling the paraffin reservoir. This was refilled every morning after extinguishing the light, by whichever man was on duty.

Marshall had only had four hours' sleep but got up at 10 a.m. and decided to go up to the tower to assist Ducat in cleaning the lens, which was a time-consuming job. Before going up, Marshall had a cup of tea and chatted to Macarthur while he drank his tea. Macarthur had cleared away the breakfast items and washed up. As an OLK Macarthur did not know either Ducat or Marshall particularly well, but he was happy to chat whenever he could, as it would not be long before he returned to Breasclete.

Their lunch was taken at 1 p.m. sharp with James Ducat keen to adhere as strictly as possible to all timings. As the meal was eaten, with a large quantity of hot soup being consumed, the talk turned to the dreadful weather of the past week. The wind and driving rain that accompanied some of the larger waves appeared to be increasing in strength. The wind could be heard and the rain seen through the kitchen window which faced south. As they ate, a heated argument arose when Ducat brought up the issue of the effect the waves and wind may have had on the equipment and box of ropes down by the west landing. It had been over two days since they had checked that everything was secure and the waves and wind had made it virtually impossible to check the west landing in safety. James Ducat wanted Macarthur to accompany him, despite the fact that Macarthur was duty cook and would have to clear away the lunch items and wash up before making preparations for teatime following a rest in the afternoon. The volatile Macarthur refused. Marshall was concerned about the waves, as he had regularly seen them swamp virtually the whole side of the west landing right to the top of the steps leading up from the landing. Ducat had also observed the waves both in the Flannans and at previous postings and was well aware of the danger. However, what was pressing heavily on his thoughts was the communication addressed to him personally the previous April from the Secretary of the Northern Lighthouse Board, James Murdoch.

Thomas Marshall also did not need reminding about the letter concerning damage to the crane on the west landing, for which he was found to be at fault and, by extension, Ducat as PLK in charge of the station. Although the letter was addressed to Ducat, the letter expressly instructed him to pass on the contents to the other lightkeepers under his command, one of whom, of course, was Thomas Marshall. Both men were in a quandary about the issue. Neither would want to put his life at risk to check that a box of ropes and other equipment including the crane were safe and had not been damaged. Whilst damage to the crane could not be avoided owing to its fixed position, the box of ropes was another matter, as it could be argued that the three of them on the station were aware of the potential effects of the sea on the west landing and any damage or loss to equipment there could be construed as negligence on their part, with accompanying disciplinary measures, including fines, against them.

The matter was discussed back and forth over their lunch, primarily between Marshall and Ducat with the odd interjection by Macarthur. However, despite failing to reach a satisfactory conclusion, both Marshall and Ducat, having discussed potential damage, loss and possible subsequent recriminations, and weighing it all up against the danger presented by the turbulent sea, felt that they would be unable to rest easily until they had gone down to the west landing to check that everything was secure. Both men felt that the gale which had been raging was still growing in strength and that it would be prudent to try and check the west landing in case anything needed to be secured before the weather worsened. Although they could still observe large waves from the light tower and the kitchen and bedroom windows, they all three wondered if the intensity of the gale had maybe passed its worst, with breaks appearing in the stormy looking clouds. All of them then went outside to observe the height of the water which came out of a blowhole, located not far from the building. The height of the water shooting out of the blowhole always gave a good indication of the force and size of the waves hitting the west landing.

After watching over a period of forty minutes from the shelter of the building, despite one or two jets of water spraying out from the blowhole to a great height, Ducat nodded to Marshall and Macarthur and suggested that the height of the water being ejected seemed to be scaling down from the past few days. Marshall agreed with him and they went to get their outside wear for the bad weather after having a quick cup of tea to warm themselves before fully venturing out. Macarthur felt relieved in one respect that he did not have to be involved in hauling the heavy box of ropes and other equipment around the west landing area in what was still foul weather, but he was still angry, as Ducat had nominated him to first polish the metalwork in the light tower before he went to get his head down in the late afternoon and then rising to start preparing their tea as duty cook. After finishing their mugs of tea, Ducat put on his sea boots and his old waterproof coat. Marshall also donned his sea boots but, unlike Ducat, he had a proper oilskin, which was probably the best item of wear against the wild elements outside the station. Macarthur heard the outside door close as the two men left before their voices were cut off by the sound of the wind and rain outside as they shut the door and started to walk towards the west landing.

As the two men approached the edge of the grassy area at the top of the rocky cliffs above the west landing, Ducat first noticed that the set of railings which started at the top were a strange shape. As they got closer they noted the turf appeared to have been ripped up to reveal the soil beneath the grass, as if a giant hand had ripped up the grass at the edge where the grass met the cliff. The metal railings were completely twisted at the point where they started. Where they led along the cliff edge and then down alongside the steps, some parts of the railings stood as normal and others were twisted and pulled from their foundations, as if a bad tempered giant had punched them with his fist and pulled at them as he had walked along. The damage was breathtaking and as Ducat and Marshall surveyed the scene at the top of the cliff edge, both men were overawed at the damage but also at the sheer massive force of the waves that must have reached up well over 100ft to cause such damage. Ducat's heart sank when he looked down the steps and saw that a lifebelt had been torn from the railings and had disappeared completely. Wordlessly he pointed it out to Marshall, who merely nodded. Over the wind and rain both men started to talk about how the news would be taken by headquarters in 84 George Street, Edinburgh. The stormy weather that they had endured over a number of days did not appear to be abating. It had not been an overly violent storm, probably nearer gale force, but the wave which had reached up and caused such damage must have occurred two nights previously when none of the men would have seen what had happened. The area was difficult to observe unless it was being directly watched from either just outside the station building or the light tower itself. As the two men proceeded down the slippery steps Ducat told Marshall that they could not obviously be held responsible for the damage to the railings and turf but the lifebelt was a different matter as it could be argued that it had not been secured properly by them.

As they passed the place where the lifebelt had originally been placed on the railings, they came to the area of the crane. The crane itself was undamaged by the force of the sea, but the metal railings had been torn away, which made both men consider what would have happened to anyone standing on the platform. They would have been totally powerless against the tons of water which must have come down from behind them as the wave washed back and swept over the platform, tearing and twisting the metal from the platform. It was still precarious there as the waves continued to break against the west landing, with the tops of the waves and the spray reaching up to the level of the crane, higher than where the two men were standing. Despite the waves obliterating the lower part of the landing, Ducat and Marshall could both see that the handrails down there, which were used for mooring and making fast the visiting boats, had been completely carried away by the mountainous seas.

As they watched the waves below on the actual landing, Ducat nudged Marshall and pointed along the path built into the rock just below them which led to the last set of steps down to the lower landing. A rope was wrapped around a rock and was partially caught up on part of a twisted railing on the lower set of steps. Some of the larger waves were breaking on this area and each time they hit, they tugged at the rope and the rope would sway but still hold its position on the rail and rock, as if refusing to give way and be sucked into the sea. Marshall, feeling some responsibility for involving Ducat in the admonition after the crane incident, said to Ducat he would go down and free the rope from the rock and pull it back up. Ducat nodded and Marshall started to make his way down over the rocks. He was younger than James Ducat but the seaboots and oilskins made movement awkward. It was slippery and the waves were breaking over the area but not so much that they presented a serious threat to his safety. It seemed a reasonable gamble to take. However, as Marshall grabbed the rope, he appeared to pull back and lose his balance, falling backwards and down into the turbulent water. Marshall disappeared under the surface but reappeared quickly, shouting and waving his arms.

Ducat realised that on his own he would be unlikely to haul Marshall out of the water so he shouted to him that he was going to run back and get Macarthur and they would pull him out. Ducat ran back up the steps and then alongside the tramway up to the station. He flew through the door and found Macarthur in the kitchen putting away the remaining utensils from lunch after washing up. Ducat shouted that there had been an accident and Marshall had fallen into the sea, and the two of them ran back out of the station. With Macarthur only dressed in his working gear and shirtsleeves, he was able to run faster than Ducat. They both made their way down to the west landing and Ducat pointed out the rope that Marshall had been trying to free, saying that they could use it to throw to Marshall, who in the intervening minutes had drifted further out to sea. The waves were up to 30ft in height and were crashing around them as they freed the rope and made their way slightly further down the rocks to be in a better position to throw the line to Marshall and then, with the strength of two men, haul him in. Ducat pondered the idea as he made his way down the rocks whether an option might be to take off his gear and tie the rope around his waist while he swam out to Marshall, but he worried whether Macarthur would have the strength to haul them both in. With Marshall in the water, facing Ducat and Macarthur, and a drenched Ducat and Macarthur preoccupied with tying the rope around Ducat's waist to act as an anchor while they threw the rope out, none of the men saw a gigantic wall of water around 60–70ft high fast approaching them.

There was a brief moment of quiet as the trough preceding the giant wave added a surreal moment of peace to the scene. Sensing the danger, both Ducat and Marshall looked up at the wall of water towering above them before it hit with tremendous and overwhelming power.

Notes

1 Reconstruction is based on Walter Albert's theory.
2 NLB Register of Lightkeepers Scottish National Archives File NLC4/1.
3 Ibid.
4 Ibid.
5 Account of visit by a minister to Flannan Isles Lighthouse, April 1900, in *Scotsman* 29 December 1900.

4

DISCOVERY

Probably the first notification that all was not well on Eilean Mor would have been the arrival of the *Archtor* at Leith, scheduled for 17 December 1900, when Captain Holman could have notified the authorities, and the Northern Lighthouse Board headquarters in Edinburgh, of the lack of a light when the ship passed the Flannan Isles less than two days previously.[1] However, the last quarter of the year 1900 was not a good one for the *Archtor*. Only six weeks prior to passing the Flannan Isles on the night of 15–16 December, the ship had suffered a broken tailshaft. On 5 November 1900 she was towed into Halifax, Nova Scotia, by the tank steamer *Chesapeake* after drifting helplessly 250 miles from Halifax bound for New York from Leith.[2] Despite the ignominy of being treated as salvage on that occasion, the reason for the delay of the *Archtor*'s arrival into Leith and an earlier reporting of the lack of an operating light on Eilean Mor was a far more serious matter. As the *Archtor* made her way in towards the Firth of Forth, the lights of the following were all visible to assist her passage: the Fidra Light; the North Carr Light Vessel; the May Island Light and finally the Anstruther Light. While the ship was between Girdleness and the Bell Rock on a south-south-westerly course, Captain Holman had taken an observation at approximately 1.45 p.m. on the afternoon of 17 December.

At approximately 4.45 p.m. the Bell Rock was passed to the west and an hour later (5.45 p.m.) the North Carr Light Vessel was abeam at a distance of approximately ¾ mile to 1 mile. Some time prior to this, Captain Holman had decided that all was proceeding well and left the bridge to go down below with the chief officer for their tea. The *Archtor* was left in the hands of the third officer. Captain Holman returned to the bridge at approximately 5.50 p.m. and was informed by the third officer that they had just passed the North Carr Light Vessel and that he had just run a four-point bearing to estimate the North Carr Light Vessel's distance from the *Archtor*. This bearing was later found to be incorrect through not taking into account the actual speed of the ship and also not taking into account the wind and tide.[3] By the time Captain Holman had returned to the bridge, it was very dark but clear. there was a moderate gale from the west-south-west and the sea conditions were slight to moderate.

Not realising that the earlier bearing made by the Third Officer was incorrect, only five minutes after his return to the bridge at 5.50 p.m., Captain Holman made the first of two relatively quick changes to the *Archtor*'s course. The first alteration was to set a south-west by westerly course allowing a full quarter of a point for easterly deviation. The ship continued on this course for ten minutes before Captain Holman made another alteration to the course by changing it to west-south-west. After five minutes on this new course, the *Archtor* struck the Carphie Rock, receiving a glancing blow on her forefoot, riding up and becoming partially stranded but not actually stopping her forward motion. She rose up and listed over to port and the speed was checked by 1½ knots. Captain Holman tried to correct the list by turning the helm to starboard and ordered a sounding of the tanks fore and aft. The sounding found that water was coming in so fast that due to the pressure of air in the sounding pipes it was difficult to take a proper sounding in the forehold and the foretank. Within an hour the engine room bilges began to fill with water. The *Archtor* had cleared the Carphie Rock but in the process had been severely damaged and was now taking on water at a rate the crew was barely containing. After keeping the ship stood out in the water at a distance of ¾ mile from the shore, Captain Holman made a quick decision to continue on towards Inchkeith Light. By this stage, the head of the *Archtor* was down towards the waterline and, due to the angle of the ship, the propeller was partially out of the water. This meant the ship was only making a speed of 4–5 knots (i.e. less than half its normal speed). Whilst the pumps on board were able to cope with keeping the water down in the engine room and the No. 2 hold, they could not cope with the level of water coming into either No. 1 hold or the collision compartment or the forepeak. Finally, at 11 p.m. that evening, at what must have been an agonising few hours of uncertainty, Captain Holman steered the *Archtor* just off the pier heads at Leith Harbour. Fortunately it was high tide and Captain Holman was able to beach the ship there at the high water mark. The *Archtor* lay forlornly in the mud for five days before being lightened and brought into Leith Harbour under her own steam.

The *Archtor*, despite suffering considerable damage, had still managed to limp her way to Leith very late on the night of 17 December and the following day Captain Holman had to account for what had happened under his command; he made known to the vessel's agents in Leith that same day (18 December) his concern at the complete absence of the light on the Flannan Islands. Even taking on the seriousness of a problem with the lighthouse not working, nobody could have realised there were far more serious implications than just a malfunction of some kind with the light.

Considering the fact that the ship initially ran aground on the Carphie Rock, near Anstruther, on 17 December 1900,[4] less than forty-eight hours after passing the Flannan Isles, Captain Holman therefore had more serious and pressing matters to attend to, not least being the possible complete loss of the ship and also his livelihood as a consequence of the grounding under his command. It would not have been unreasonable to expect him to put the matter of the missing light completely out of his mind for some time. Furthermore, all he could have seen was that the Flannan Isles light was not working and it may not have been working for any number of reasons. He could not have had any inkling of the calamity that had taken place there. Despite the not inconsiderable problems facing Captain Holman, he arrived in Leith on 18 December 1900 (only a day later than intended) and notified his concern about the failure of the Eilean Mor light that same day to the *Archtor*'s owners (Henderson and McIntosh). A letter from Henderson and McIntosh was eventually sent on 28 December 1900 to the secretary of the NLB informing them of Captain Holman's observations and apologising for the delay in notification, but referred to the grounding of the *Archtor* as the reason for preoccupying them.[5] It must be said that this was more for information only, as by 28 December 1900 everyone was becoming aware of the unfolding tragedy on the Flannan Isles. The final paragraph of the letter states: 'We should have brought this matter under your notice previously, but having been so much occupied by the accident to this steamer and other affairs, the matter escaped our memory.'[6]

Captain Holman's immediate decision after striking the Carphie Rock – to continue onwards towards the Inchkeith Light and his final destination, Leith – was commended by the later court of inquiry, but he was severely reprimanded for the incident itself and warned to be more careful in future. He had come very close to having his Master's Certificate withdrawn.[7] The *Archtor* herself was finally sailed around to Sunderland where the £4,000 worth of damage caused by the collision with the Carphie Rock was repaired. Despite the problem the *Archtor* faced, in many ways the vessel and her crew were fortunate that the problem was not as serious as it could have been – that is, the complete sinking of the vessel.

The other quarter where an earlier notification of the failure of the light may have been expected to come from was the NLB's lookout on Gallan Head on Lewis. Just prior to the official establishment of the Eilean Mor Lighthouse, NLB Superintendent Robert Muirhead recommended the appointment of Roderick MacKenzie, a gamekeeper of Uig. MacKenzie lived in a house near Gallan Head, the closest point on Lewis to the Eilean Mor Lighthouse. Despite the lighthouse being 20 miles away, it was felt that it was still the best location for observations of signals from the lighthouse. Muirhead had met MacKenzie, and his view was that he was an intelligent man and ably assisted by his two sons, who were also gamekeepers. Their skills at deerstalking, which involved considerable observation of distant objects using glasses, made them ideal observers for the NLB. In a letter dated 27 December 1899, the Board of Trade gave their approval for Roderick Mackenzie to be appointed at a salary of £8 per annum, with the proviso that at the end of twelve months a report was to be sent to them showing how efficient the signalling communication was, to aid them in calculating the average number of days on which it was used.

The system of signalling itself was by use of discs which were hung on poles from either side of the balcony on top of the lighthouse tower. The signals were differentiated by one or more discs being hung from different sides of the lighthouse tower. The primary purpose of the signalling system was to enable Mackenzie, and thereby the NLB, to be informed when assistance was required by the lighthouse.

A powerful telescope[8] which had originally been presented to the Lighthouse Commissioners (as the NLB were also known) by Lloyds was sent to Mackenzie, who officially started his observation duties on 1 February 1900, ten and a half months before the tragedy.

The failure of the *Archtor*'s agents, Henderson and McIntosh, to notify the NLB of Captain Holman's observations and concerns until their letter dated 28 December 1900, plus no notification from Roderick Mackenzie on Lewis, meant that all was assumed to be well at the Eilean Mor

Lighthouse up until 26 December 1900 (Captain Holman had passed the Flannan Islands on 15–16 December and reported to the *Archtor's* owners on 18 December 1900). There was therefore a ten-day gap between Captain Holman informing Henderson and McIntosh, and them in turn informing the NLB headquarters.

Eilean Mor was one of a number of the NLB's stations and lighthouses which were replenished by a relief vessel named the *Hesperus*.[9] On this occasion, the arrival of the *Hesperus* at the Flannan Isles was delayed slightly by bad weather. The vessel had left its Oban base on Monday 24 December 1900 (Christmas Eve) and made her way up to Loch Roag on Lewis to collect supplies and the relief lightkeeper, Joseph Moore, and take them out to Eilean Mor. There was bad weather in the area over this period with very strong gales, described in some accounts as a storm, over 17–21 December 1900. On 26 December 1900 the *Hesperus* finally left Loch Roag and made her way over to Eilean Mor. The first indication that something was wrong was the lack of the lighthouse flag on Eilean Mor which would show the relief vessel was expected. At first, those on the *Hesperus* assumed the lightkeepers had not seen them arriving so the steamer's horn was sounded, but there was no response. A signal rocket was fired from the *Hesperus* and after the horn was sounded again with still no response from the lighthouse, Captain Harvey decided to land a boat with a group of men including the relief keeper Moore. When the boat reached the west landing, Moore went ashore first, leaving McCormack and the others in the rowing boat while he went to investigate. Moore made his way up the steep steps of the west landing to the top of the cliff and on up to the lighthouse. When he arrived at the entrance gate to the lighthouse, he found it closed. He then went to the entrance door leading to the kitchen and stores and it too was closed, but not locked. Once inside, he found that an inner door which led into the kitchen was open. In the kitchen he saw that the fireplace had not been lit for some days. Moore must have been disturbed by what he found. He went into the rooms of each keeper which all led off from the small kitchen and found the beds were exactly as they would have been left in the early morning. He felt there and then that something serious had happened and decided to make his way back to the boat at the landing stage. Once there he informed McCormack that the lighthouse station was deserted. Moore and McCormack plus some of the men from the boat went back up to the lighthouse for another look to make certain there was nobody there.

The first notification of the tragedy to the wider world was a telegram[10] sent by Captain Harvey, the master of the *Hesperus*, to Mr Murdoch, the secretary of the NLB. The *Hesperus* returned to Loch Roag, Lewis, that same evening and the message was handed in to the telegraph office at the small village of Callanish on a headland at Loch Roag at 7.14 p.m. on 26 December 1900 and received at 8.27 p.m. by Mr Murdoch at his home, St Kilda, Trinity, Edinburgh. A copy of the same telegram was also sent to the NLB's superintendent, Robert Muirhead. The telegram from Captain Harvey read:

A dreadful accident has happened at Flannans. The three keepers Ducat, Marshall and the occasional have disappeared from the island. On our arrival there this afternoon no signs of life was to be seen on the island.

Fired a rocket, but, as no response was made, managed to land Moore, who went up to the station but found no keepers there. The clocks were stopped and other signs indicated that the accident must have happened about a week ago. Poor fellows they must have been blown over the cliffs or drowned trying to secure a crane or something like that. Night coming on, we could not wait to make further investigation, but will go off again tomorrow morning to try and learn something as to their fate. I have left Moore, MacDonald, Buoymaster, and two seamen on the Island to keep the light burning until you make other arrangements. Will not return to Oban until I hear from you. I have repeated this wire to Muirhead, in case you are not at home. I will remain at the telegraph office tonight, until it closes, if you wish to wire me.[11]

Superintendent Robert Muirhead took control of the situation and arranged for the smooth running of the Eilean Mor Lighthouse with as little disruption as possible to other stations. Nevertheless, some juggling around was necessary, given the complete loss of the staff at one station. On 8 January 1901 Muirhead made a clear and succinct report to the Lighthouse Board Commissioners on the disaster and his handling of it:[12]

> On receipt of Captain Harvie's telegram of the 26th December reporting that the three keepers on Flannan Islands, viz., James Ducat, Principal, Thomas Marshall, second Assistant, and Donald Macarthur, Occasional Keeper (doing duty for William Ross, first Assistant, on sick leave), had disappeared, and that they must have been blown over the cliffs, or drowned, I made the following arrangements with the Secretary for the temporary working of the station – James Ferrier, Principal Keeper, was sent from Stornoway Lighthouse to Tiumpan Head Lighthouse, and John Milne, Principal Keeper at Tiumpan Head was sent to take charge at Flannan Islands. Donald Jack, the second Assistant Storekeeper, was also despatched to Flannan Islands, the intention being that these two men, along with Joseph Moore, the third Assistant at Flannan Islands, who was ashore when the accident took place, should do duty pending permanent arrangements being made.
>
> I also proceeded to Flannan Islands, where I was landed, along with Milne and Jack, early on the 29th also.
>
> After satisfying myself that everything connected with the light was in good order, and that the men landed would be able to maintain the light, I proceeded to ascertain, if possible, the cause of the disaster, and also took statements

from Captain Harvie and Mr McCormack the second mate of the Hesperus, Joseph Moore third Assistant Keeper Flannan Islands, and Allan MacDonald, Buoymaster, and the following is the result of my investigations:

The Hesperus arrived at Flannan Islands for the purpose of making the ordinary relief about noon on Wednesday, the 26th December, and, as neither signals were shown, nor any of the usual preparations for landing made, Captain Harvie blew both the steam whistle and the siren to call the attention of the keepers. As this had no effect, he fired a rocket, which also evoked no response, and a boat was lowered and sent ashore to the East landing, with Joseph Moore, Assistant Keeper. When the boat reached the landing, there being still no sign of the keepers, the boat was backed into the landing, and with some difficulty Moore managed to jump ashore. When he went up to the station, he found the entrance gate and outside doors closed, the clock stopped, no fire lit, and, looking into the bedrooms, he found the beds empty. He became alarmed at this, and ran down to the boat and informed Mr McCormack, the second mate, that the keepers were missing. McCormack and one of the seamen managed to jump ashore, and with Moore made a thorough search of the Station, but could discover nothing. They then returned to the ship and informed Captain Harvie, who told Moore he would have to return to the island to keep the light going pending instructions, and called for volunteers from his crew to assist in this. He met with a ready response, and two seamen, Lamont and Campbell, were selected, and Mr McDonald, the Buoymaster, who was on board, also offered his services, which were accepted, and Moore, MacDonald and these two seamen were left in charge of the light, while Captain Harvie returned to Breascleit and telegraphed an account of the disaster to the Secretary.

The men left on the island made a thorough search, in the first place of the station, and found that the last entry on the slate had been made by Mr Ducat, the Principal Keeper on the morning of Saturday the 15th December. The lamp was trimmed, the oil fountains and canteens were filled up and the lens and machinery cleaned, which proves that the work of the forenoon of the 15th had been completed. The pots and pans had been cleaned and the kitchen tidied up, which showed that the man who had been acting as cook had completed his work, which goes to prove that the men disappeared on the afternoon of Saturday, the 15th December. This is borne out by information which was received (after news of the disaster had been published) that Captain Holman had passed the Flannan Islands in the steamer 'Archtor' at midnight on the 15th ulto., and could not observe the light, though, from the condition of the weather and his position, he felt satisfied that he should have seen it.

On the Thursday and Friday the men made a thorough search over and round the island, and I went over the ground with them on the Saturday. Everything at the East landing place was in order, and the ropes which had been coiled and stored there on the completion of the relief of the 7th December were all in their places, and the lighthouse buildings and everything at the Station was in order. Traces of the severity of the weather were, however to be found at the West landing place. Owing to the amount of sea, I could not get down to the landing place, but I got down to the crane platform, about 70 feet above the sea level. The crane originally erected on this platform was washed away during last winter, and the crane put up this Summer was found to be unharmed, the jib lowered and secured to the rock, and the canvas covering the wire rope on the barrel securely lashed around it, and there was no evidence that the men had been doing anything at the crane. The mooring ropes, landing ropes, derrick landing ropes and crane handles, as also a wooden box in which they were kept, and which was secured in a crevice in the rocks 70 feet up the tramway from its terminus, and about 40 feet higher than the crane platform, or 110 feet in all above the sea level, had been washed away, and the ropes were strewn in the crevices of the rocks near the crane platform and entangled among the crane legs, but they were all coiled up, no single coil being found unfastened. The iron railings round the crane platform and from the terminus of the tramway to the concrete steps up from the West landing were displaced and twisted. A large block of stone, weighing upwards of 20cwt had been dislodged from its position higher up and carried down to and left on the concrete path leading from the terminus of the tramway to the top of the steps. A life buoy fastened to the railings along this path, to be used in case of emergency, had disappeared, and I thought at first that it had been removed for the purpose of being used, but, on examining the ropes by which it was fastened, I found that they had not been touched, and as pieces of canvas were adhering to the ropes, it was evident that the force of the sea pouring through the railings had, even at this great height (110 feet above sea level) torn the lifebuoy off the ropes.

When the accident occurred, Ducat was wearing sea boots and a waterproof, and Marshall sea boots and oilskins, and as Moore assures me that the men only wore those articles when going down to the landings, they must have intended, when they left the station, either to go down to the landing or the proximity of it.

After a careful examination of the place, the railings, ropes, etc., and weighing all the evidence which I could secure, I am of opinion that the most likely explanation of the disappearance of the men is that they had all gone down on the afternoon of Saturday, the 15th December, to the proximity of the west landing, to secure the box with the mooring ropes, etc., and that an unexpectedly large roller had come up on the island, and a large body of water going up higher than where they were and coming down upon them had swept them away with resistless force. I have considered and discussed the possibility of the men being blown away by the wind, but, as the wind was westerly, I am of opinion, notwithstanding its great force, that the more probable explanation is that they have been washed away, as, had the wind caught them, it would, from its direction, have blown them up the island, and I feel certain that they would have managed to throw themselves down before they reached the summit or brow of the island.

On the conclusion of my enquiry on Saturday afternoon, I returned to Breascleit, wired the result of my investigations to the Secretary, and called on the widows of James Ducat, the Principal Keeper, and Donald Macarthur, the Occasional Keeper.

I may state that, as Moore was naturally very much upset by the unfortunate occurrence, and appeared very nervous, I left A. Lamont, seaman, on the Island to go to the lightroom and keep Moore company when on watch for a week or two. If this nervousness does not leave Moore, he will require to be transferred, but I am reluctant to recommend this, as I would desire to have one man at least who knows the work of the Station. The Commissioners appointed Roderick MacKenzie, Gamekeeper, Uig, near Meavsig, to look out daily for signals that might be shown from the rock, and to note each night whether the light was seen or not seen. As it was evident that the light had not been lit from the 15th to the 26th of December, I resolved to see him on Sunday morning, to ascertain what he had to say on the subject. He was from home, but I found his two sons, aged about 18 and 16 – two most intelligent lads of the gamekeeper class, and who actually perform the duty of looking out for the signals – and had a conversation with them on the matter, and I also examined the Return Book. From the December Return, I saw that the tower itself was not seen, even with the assistance of a powerful telescope, between the 7th and the 29th of December. The light was, however, seen on the 7th December but was not seen on the 8th, 9th, 10th and 11th. It was seen on the 12th, but was not seen again until the 26th, the night on which it was lit by Moore. Mackenzie stated (and I have since verified this), that the light sometimes cannot be seen for four or five consecutive nights, but he was beginning to be anxious at not seeing it for such a long period, and had, for two nights prior to its reappearance, been getting the assistance of the natives to see if it could be discerned.

Had the lookout been kept by an ordinary lightkeeper, as at Earraid for Dhuheartach, I believe it would have struck the man ashore at an earlier period that something was amiss, and, while this would not have prevented the lamentable occurrence taking place, it would have enabled steps to have be taken to have had the light relit at an earlier stage.

I would recommend that the Signalman should be instructed that, in future, should he fail to observe the light when, in his opinion, looking to the state of the atmosphere, it should be seen, he should be instructed to intimate this to the secretary, when the propriety of taking steps could be considered.

I may explain that signals are shown from Flannan Islands by displaying balls or discs from each side of the Tower, on poles projecting out from the lighthouse balcony, the signals being differentiated by one or more discs being shown on the different sides of the Tower.

When at Flannan Islands so lately as the 7th December last, I had a conversation with the late Mr Ducat regarding the signals, and he stated that he wished it would be necessary to hoist one of the signals, just to ascertain how long it would be seen ashore and how soon it would be acted upon.

At that time, I took a note to consider the propriety of having a signal to say that all was well – signals under the present system being only exhibited when assistance of some kind is required. After carefully considering the matter, and discussing it with the officials competent to offer an opinion on the subject, I arrived at the conclusion that it would not be advisable to have such a signal, as, owing to the distance between the island and the shore, and to the frequency of haze on top of the island, it would often be unseen for such a duration of time as to cause alarm, especially on the part of the keepers' wives and families and I would point out that no day signals could have been seen between the 7th and 29th December, and an 'All Well' signal would have been of no use on this occasion.

The question has been raised as to how we would have been situated had wireless telegraphy been instituted, but, had we failed to establish communication for some days, I should have concluded that something had gone wrong with the signalling apparatus, and the last thing that would have occurred to me would have been that all the three men had disappeared.

In conclusion I would desire to record my deep regret at such a disaster occurring to keepers in this Service. I knew Ducat and Marshall intimately, and Macarthur, the Occasional, well. They were selected on my recommendation, for the lighting of such an important Station as Flannan Islands, and as it is always my endeavour to secure the best men possible for the establishment of a Station, as the success and contentment at a Station depends largely on the Keepers present at its installation, this of itself is an indication that the Board has lost two of its most efficient Keepers and a competent Occasional. I was with the Keepers for more than a month during the summer of 1899, when everyone worked hard to secure the early lighting of the Station before winter, and, working along with them, I appreciated the manner in which they performed their work. I visited Flannan Islands when the relief was made as lately as the 7th December, and have the melancholy recollection that I was the last person to shake hands with them and bid them adieu.

Robert Muirhead
Superintendent
8th January 1901[13]

It can be assumed that Muirhead wrote the report whilst he was on Eilean Mor. He arrived on 29 December (with replacement lightkeeper Milne and storesman Jack) and the report is dated ten days later (8 January 1901). However, it is more likely that having made a thorough search of the island and the station itself, Muirhead returned to 84 George Street, Edinburgh. He would have been more likely to have written-up his report at 84 George Street where he had administrative support, could call any witnesses (Edinburgh being easier than the Flannan Isles for travel) and more importantly would have had immediate access to lawyers should he have felt their advice needed to be sought. One other strong possibility is that when Muirhead left Eilean Mor to return to Edinburgh, he took the logbook with him so he could consult it while he was preparing the report. The logbooks were sacrosanct records and it would seem inconceivable that Muirhead would have left it there, as it contained the records written in the missing men's own hand up until the day they disappeared. Rather than just leave it to continue being used at the station, it would have formed documentary evidence for the investigation and it would have been easy enough for Muirhead to arrange for a new one to be used at Eilean Mor from the takeover by the replacement lightkeepers. It may also help to explain why the logbook has disappeared. With its removal from Eilean Mor rather than just allowing it to be completed and returned in the normal course for filing away in archives, Muirhead may have felt that as it was the primary document relating to the tragedy, it should be kept separately from the archives in case anyone wished to consult it. It is possible that the letter sent by the Crown Office to the NLB (*see Chapter 7*) on 1 February 1901 may have included a request to see the logbook, and with the passing out of the book for inspection, and with the passing of time, it has either been mislaid or filed away somewhere and forgotten over the years.

Muirhead's report is the most comprehensive account of the uncovering of the tragedy. It was written with the benefit of immediacy (almost two weeks after the discovery of the missing keepers) and the fact that Muirhead himself acted as the main investigator. It could be argued that at least one other independent investigator may have been able to add something to the mystery, but Muirhead was the Board's superintendent and with his background and intimate knowledge he would have been the best placed, in any event, to undertake the investigation and write the report. However, almost as important, as he was literally first on the scene, is the much shorter report sent to the NLB Secretary by the ALK Joseph Moore. Moore's report was written on 28 December 1900, only two days after the discovery of the missing keepers. Written on Flannan Islands Lighthouse headed paper, he states:[14]

Sir,
It's with deep regret I wish you to learn the very sad affair which has taken place here during the past fortnight; namely the disappearance of my poor fellow Lighthouse Keepers Mr Ducat and Mr Marshall together with the occasional Keeper Donald Macarthur from off this island.

As you are aware the relief was here on 26th. That day as on other relief days, we came to anchorage under Flannan Islands, and not seeing the lighthouse flag flying we thought they did not perceive us coming. The steamer's horn was sounded several times. Still no reply. At last Captain Harvey deemed it prudent to lower a boat and land a man if it was possible. I was the first to land leaving Mr McCormack and his men in the boat till I should return from the lighthouse. I went up and on coming to the entrance gate, I found it closed. I made for entrance door leading to the kitchen and store and I found it also closed and the door inside that, but the kitchen door was open. On entering the kitchen I looked at the fireplace and saw that the fire was not lighted for some days. I then entered the rooms in succession, found the beds empty, just as they left them in the early morning. I did not take time to search further. For I only too well knew that something serious had occurred. I darted out and made for the landing. When I reached there I informed Mr McCormack that the place was deserted. He with some of the men came up a second time so as to make sure, but unfortunately the first impression was only too true.

Mr McCormack and myself proceeded to the lighthouse, where everything was left in proper order. The lantern was cleaned. The fountain full. Blinds on the windows etc. We left and proceeded on board the steamer. On arrival Captain Harvey ordered me back again to the island accompanied with Mr McDonald (Buoymaster), A Campbell and A Lamont who were to do duty with me till timely aid should arrive. We went on shore and proceeded on to [the] Lightroom and lighted the light in its proper times that night and every night since. The following day we traversed the island from end to end but still nothing to see to convince us how it happened. Nothing appears touched at [the] east landing to show that they were taken from there. Ropes are all in their respective places in the shelter just as they were left after [the] relief on 7th [December]. On West Side it is somewhat different. We had an old box half way up the railway for holding West landing mooring ropes and tackle, and it has gone. Some of the ropes it appears got washed out of it, they lie strewn on the rocks near the crane. The crane itself is safe.

The iron railings along the passage connecting [the] railway with footpath to landing are started from their foundations and broken in several places. Also railing round crane and hand rail for making mooring ropes fast for boats is entirely carried away. Now there is nothing to give us an indication that of course there the poor men lost their lives, only that Mr Marshall had his sea-boots on and oilskin also. Mr Ducat has his sea-boots on. He had no oilskin, only an old waterproof coat and that is away. Donald Macarthur has his wearing coat left behind him which shows us, far as I know, that he went out in shirt sleeves. He never used any other coat on previous occasions only the one I am reffering [sic] to.

From the monthly return it is recorded they are missing since 15th. Up till 13th is marked in the book and 14th is marked on [the] slate along with part of 15th. On 14th the prevailing state of the weather was (dividing sign) westerly olb bry shrs. On 15th the hour of extinguishing [the light] was noted on slate along with barometer and thermometer inside and outside lantern taken at (9am) as usual and direction of wind. The kitchen utensils were all very clean, which is a sign that it must be after dinner some time that they left. There is one thing I know that Mr Marshall never wore sea boots or oilskins only taken in connection with landings.

I Remain Sir
Your Obedient Servant
JOP Moore[15]

At first glance, it would largely appear that the grammar in Moore's letter/report is somewhat stilted. In those days, and for some considerable time into the twentieth century, lightkeepers were regarded very much as 'blue-collar' workers – educated, of course, but not to 'professional' standards. That much remained unchanged right through to the 1970s and beyond. In addition, Moore would have been under considerable stress and pressure to get something on paper with the least possible delay. An NLB employee at his level would not be used to communicating with higher authority. Such communications would normally have been the prerogative of the principal lighthouse keeper. Promotion was much slower in those days, a strict protocol would have been observed, with a much greater respect for the chain of command than would have been the case later.

It should also be remembered that the discovery of the missing keepers had had a profoundly unsettling effect on Moore. So much so that although Muirhead had left him as one of the temporary staff manning the Eilean Mor Lighthouse, he had commented in his report that Moore's state of nervousness and agitation was worrying and that he would have to consider removing him from the Flannan Isles if he did not improve.

After going through both Moore's short report of his immediate findings and Muirhead's longer report of his investigation, two things are very clear which refute two of the myths that constantly circulate about this mystery. The first myth is the uneaten meal lying on the table. Moore as first on the scene states: 'The kitchen utensils were all very clean, which is a sign that it must be after dinner some time that they left.'[16] Then Muirhead's report, written only eleven days later, states in a similar vein: 'The pots and pans had been cleaned and the kitchen tidied up, which showed that the man who had been acting as cook had completed his work.'[17]

The second myth is often mentioned and appears to heighten the 'drama' of the disappearance is the entries in the station log and on the slate prior to entry in the log. Although Robert Muirhead makes no actual reference to either the station log or the slate, it is impossible to believe that he would have ignored such 'dramatic' entries and made no reference to them. The supposed entries were said to be written in Thomas Marshall's hand in the dramatic prose style of Victorian times and state:

> Dec. 12th Gale, north by north-west. Sea lashed to fury. Stormbound 9 p.m. Never seen such a storm. Everything shipshape. Ducat irritable. 12 p.m. Storm still raging. Wind Steady. Stormbound. Cannot go out. Ship passed sounding foghorn. Could see lights of cabins. Ducat quiet. Macarthur crying.

> Dec. 13th Storm continued through night. Wind shifted west by north. Ducat quiet. Macarthur praying. 12 noon. Grey daylight. Me, Ducat and Macarthur prayed.

Dec. 15th 1 p.m. Storm ended. Sea calm. God is over all.

These entries first came to prominence in a book written by an American writer named Vincent Hayes Gaddis. Gaddis was born in 1913 in Ohio, USA. He died in February 1997. He had been a newspaper reporter and writer-editor for a radio station in Indiana before becoming a feature writer for the *Elkhart Truth*, a daily newspaper in Elkhart, Indiana. He had then gone on to work as a public relations writer for the Studebaker-Packard Corporation and Mercedes-Benz Sales in South Bend, Indiana. In 1962 he turned to full-time writing and eventually had a number of books published. He is best-known for coining the term Bermuda Triangle in a cover piece for the *Argosy* journal in February 1964.

The genre that Gaddis specialised in was anomalous phenomena (phenomena for which there is no explanation in a specific body of scientific knowledge) and he was heavily influenced by Charles Hoy Fort, an earlier American writer who specialised in anomalous phenomena. In 1965 Gaddis had a book published entitled *Invisible Horizons: True Mysteries of the Sea* in which he related the loss of the three Flannan Isles lightkeepers. In his book, Gaddis recounts the above logbook entries supposedly written by Thomas Marshall and attributes the source for the logbook entries to an article in an August 1929 pulp fiction magazine called *Strange True Stories*. The article had been written by American pulp fiction writer Ernest Fallon, and he gave as his source for the entries 'English Sources'. The use of 'English' is fairly telling as, although Fallon was American and he probably would have used the word 'English' to cover Britain and Scotland, the matter was a purely Scottish affair with little English input. It seems highly unlikely that any log entry of the type above would have been notified to, or come into the possession of, anyone in England. Even cosidering the possibility that there had been a diary kept by Thomas Marshall and this diary had been found and kept by one of the party searching the Flannans Lighthouse, it is very unlikely that it would have made its way to England without having come to prominence in Scotland first. Furthermore, any Scottish source would never have described themselves as English.

In those days, a subordinate would not have written such comments about his superior without the risk of a serious reprimand and it is extremely unlikely that he would have written in the official logbook that his superior was 'irritable'. Neither did the storm end at 1 p.m. on 15 December and the sea become 'calm'. The wind and sea were still building up at that point to reach just below storm force five hours later.

Once it became apparent that the lighthouse station was deserted, it would be logical that the first thing Muirhead and Moore would have looked for would be an indication of when the lightkeepers may have disappeared. The station log and the slate would have been the most obvious place to look, as they were updated on a daily basis, and so it proved to be with the weather and light times for the 14 and 15 December 1900 noted on the slate. The logbook entries for 12 and 13 December would already have been in the logbook not the slate, and the PLK, James Ducat, would have been responsible for transferring the information from the slate into the official logbook, not Thomas Marshall, an ALK. Whilst the hierarchy and duties of ALKs and PLKs may have eased slightly in later years in the twentieth century, in 1900 they would have been far more rigidly formal and strictly adhered to.

Joseph Moore, in his brief report[18] dated 28 December 1900 to the NLB Secretary, quite clearly states:

> From the monthly return it is recorded they are missing since 15th. Up till 13th is marked in the book and 14th is marked on (the) slate along with part of 15th. On 14th the prevailing state of the weather was: westerly oh by 1 hrs. On 15th the hour of extinguishing (the light) was noted on slate along with barometer and thermometer inside and outside lantern taken at (9am) as usual and direction of wind.[19]

The conclusion reached by Muirhead for his report was that the three men had perished on the west landing.

There are two possible main conclusions which an independent observer can make about these 'dramatic' log book entries not being mentioned by Moore and Muirhead. The first is that they were made by Thomas Marshall and that they were seen by both Moore and Muirhead, but they decided that no good would be served in any way by making the information public, or Muirhead as superintendent made this decision himself and instructed Moore to keep the information to himself. This is an extremely unlikely scenario. Muirhead would have been well aware at an early stage that the authorities would have been involved in the investigation of three strange deaths with the possibility of a Court Inquiry and he would have been putting his own position at considerable risk by withholding evidence in any way. The NLB superintendents had reputations as formidable and principled men and whatever had happened on Eilean Mor on 15 December 1900 would have had no direct bearing on the reputation of Muirhead himself. Equally, whilst it could be argued that Muirhead may have removed the logbook to somehow spare the reputation of the NLB in case it showed anything that may have cast the Commissioners in a bad light (no pun intended), this is, again, improbable. After seeing the damage caused by the giant wave or waves, Muirhead appears to have made his mind up that that is how the men disappeared.

The strange supposed entries by Marshall concerning the behaviour of the other two, the storm and the three of them praying with the storm finishing, ended at 1 p.m. on 15 December with the words 'God is over all', implying that all three of them were alive once the dreadful storm had finished.

Another conclusion that can be reached is that the entries were complete and utter nonsense, dreamt up by a pulp fiction writer who could not or would not identify his supposed 'English Sources', probably because they never existed in the first place. Following on from this, these false entries have entered the lore of the story without being questioned over the years.

Finally, the 'overturned chair' that is sometimes mentioned actually comes from the poem 'Flannan Isle', like the uneaten meal.

Notes

1 Captain Holman's statement, of passing the Flannan Isles on 15–16 December 1900, 29 December 1900, Scottish National Archives file no. NLC3/1/1. It is erroneously reported in some accounts that the *Archtor* docked at Oban after passing the Flannan Isles on 15–16 December 1900, but this is not the case. The voyage was listed as Philadelphia–Leith. It would have been impossible for the *Archtor*, having sailed past the Flannan Isles down to Oban, docked and then set sail for Leith around the north of Scotland, to have grounded herself on the Carphie Rock on 17 December 1900 in that time frame. Finally the court inquiry held on 22–23 January 1901 (report no. 6137) makes no mention of Oban.
2 Article 'Rescued a Steamer at Sea', 6 November 1900, *New York Times*.
3 Court inquiry, Sunderland 22–23 January 1901, report no. 6137 published by Board of Trade, 8 February 1901. Holman was aware there was a problem with the compasses on the vessel and used deviation cards, but after being absent for six months from the *Archtor*, only arriving back to take command in November 1900, there is certainly an argument he should have taken greater care.
4 Ibid.
5 Letter from Henderson and McIntosh to the Secretary, Northern Lighthouse Board, Edinburgh, Scottish National Archives file no. NL/3/1/1.
6 Ibid.
7 Court inquiry, Sunderland 22–23 January 1901, report no. 6137 published by Board of Trade, 8 February 1901.
8 The magnification of the telescope is not mentioned – only that it was 'powerful'. Scottish National Archives file no. NL/3/1/1.
9 *Hesperus* was a steel twin-screw steamer built in 1896 and eventually broken up in 1940 by Clayton & Davie Ltd, Dunston-on-Tyne.
10 Copy of text of telegram from Captain Harvey, Scottish National Archive file no. NLC3/1/1. Harvey's name is spelt as Harvie/Harvey in various accounts.

11 Ibid.
12 Report by Superintendent Robert Muirhead on disaster at Flannan Isles Lighthouse, dated 8 January 1901, Scottish National Archive file no. NLC3/1/1.
13 Ibid.
14 Report to secretary of NLB by Joseph Moore, assistant lighthouse keeper, 28 December 1900, Scottish National Archives file no. NL/3/1/1.
15 Ibid.
16 Ibid.
17 Report by Superintendent Robert Muirhead on disaster at Flannan Isles Lighthouse, 8 January 1901, Scottish National Archive file no. NLC3/1/1.
18 Report to secretary of NLB by Joseph Moore, assistant Lighthouse Keeper, 28 December 1900, Scottish National Archives file no. NL/3/1/1.
19 Ibid.

AFTERMATH

From 26 December 1900, the two most pressing matters were to find out what had happened to the three missing lightkeepers and to ensure the smooth and continuous running of the Flannan Isles lighthouse.

As an immediate and temporary short-term measure to take some pressure off Superintendent Muirhead, the NLB secretary James Murdoch sent three telegrams on 29 December 1900.[1] The first was sent to Captain Harvey, the Master of the Light Tender *Hesperus,* care of the shore station at Breasclete, telling him to remain at Breasclete until a lightkeeper named J.N. Milne arrived from Tiumpan Head and an NLB assistant storekeeper from Granton named Donald Jack arrived at Breasclete. They were to be taken by the *Hesperus* to help at the Flannans and keep things running until Muirhead could sort out a more permanent arrangement. Murdoch instructed Captain Harvey that once he had taken these two men out to Eilean Mor, he could bring back MacDonald and Harvey's other two men. Both Assistant Storekeeper Jack and Lightkeeper Milne were expected to arrive at Breasclete late on the 30 December 1900 or the following morning ,which was a Monday, and Captain Harvey was to immediately take them out to the Flannans, return with the others to Breasclete and then send a telegram to Murdoch informing him that all his instructions had been carried out.

In order for this part of Murdoch's plan to be achieved, he sent his second telegram to Lightkeeper Ferrier at Stornoway, instructing him to immediately call in the OLK to replace him, while he in turn was to immediately proceed that day to Tiumpan Head Lighthouse to replace Milne, who Murdoch informed him, was going to the Flannan Isles station for approximately two weeks as a result of the accident there.

The third telegram sent by Murdoch was to lightkeeper J.N. Milne at Tiumpan Head and stated: 'Accident Flannan Islands. You go there take charge for fortnight or so. Meet mail steamer Stornoway tomorrow night. Jack Assistant Storekeeper, will arrive with her. Drive over together to Breascleit and join 'Hesperus'. Ferrier, Stornoway, will arrive tonight to take charge Tiumpan Head. Wire reply.'[2]

With these telegrams all sent on the same day, James Murdoch had solved the immediate problem of finding a very short term solution to the manning problem while Muirhead was still trying to piece together what had happened to the three missing lightkeepers.

The key to holding the Flannans Isles station together lay with Joseph Moore. Moore had originally been scheduled as the relief to replace Thomas Marshall for his break off the rock. He was born on 28 March 1871 and was twenty-eight years old when he entered the service of the NLBoard on 28 August 1899. Moore, of course, was the first onto Eilean Mor and had found the three men missing. As the details of the tragedy unfolded, with a search (organised by Muirhead) being made over the whole of Eilean Mor, the event had deeply unsettled Moore. As Moore walked into the lighthouse building on 26 December 1900, he had probably already surmised that neither Ducat, Marshall nor Macarthur were present. It must have felt eerie in that late winter afternoon walking through the darkened rooms which had been empty for eleven days to find no trace of his colleagues, particularly as he was alone at this point with the other men still waiting at the east landing in the boat lowered from the *Hesperus*. Had Moore arrived at the west landing it would have given him an inkling that all was not well.

After landing from the boat he would have had to walk up the steps which turned back on themselves leading to the crane platform which lay slightly down from the steps. As he walked towards the crane platform more or less directly in front of him, it would have been immediately obvious that the rails surrounding the crane had been torn out and washed away. After passing the crane platform area, the steps then turned backwards again on themselves leading to the top of the cliff edge and again Moore would have passed further damage in the form of buckled rails and torn turf at the top by the cliff edge. Another possible reason for his agitated state (*see* Muirhead's comments, below) would have been the fact that he was intimately acquainted with the Eilean Mor Lighthouse. The station with which he was very familiar must have taken on a sinister aspect, with the almost certain likelihood that deaths had occurred there. When he joined the service of the NLB on 28 August 1899, he was immediately posted to the Flannan Isles (on 2 September) as an assistant lighthouse keeper and was on the roster for Eilean Mor at the time of the disappearances, having served over one and a half years on Eilean Mor by December 1900. In his official report, dated 8 January 1901, Muirhead acknowledged Moore's nervous condition:

> I may state that, as Moore was naturally very much upset by the unfortunate occurrence, and appeared very nervous, I left A. Lamont, seaman, on the Island to go to the lightroom and keep Moore company when on watch for a week or two. If this nervousness does not leave Moore, he will require to be transferred, but I am reluctant to recommend this, as I would desire to have one man at least who knows the work of the Station.[3]

Muirhead further acknowledges in the report that whilst he was aware of Moore's mental state, he needed him on Eilean Mor, at least for the first short period after the disaster, as he knew the station and its workings intimately. This would at least give Muirhead time to reorganise and plan a new schedule/roster, as with the loss of three experienced lightkeepers it was not going to be an easy task. On 15 January 1901 Muirhead wrote a memo for the NLB Commissioners entitled 'Memorandum by the Superintendent regarding the necessity for transferring J. Moore Assistant Keeper Flannan Isles'. The memo stated:

> In my report of 8th Inst., on the Flannan Islands disaster I stated that Moore Assistant Keeper at that Station was very much upset by the unfortunate circumstances and in a high state of nervousness.
>
> When at Flannan Islands on the 29th Ulto Moore informed me that he could not remain at that Station, but on my pointing out to him the great disadvantage of having all the staff new men, he agreed to continue doing duty in the meantime, in the hope that this nervousness would wear off. I stated at the same time that under the circumstances, I felt assured that the Commissioners would not insist on his being kept there should he consider it necessary to be transferred. Moore has written me requesting a transfer, but agreeing to remain at the Flannans until the new men are up to the work of the Station. I do not consider it advisable to retain him at the Flannans, either in his own interest or in that of the Station, and would recommend that A. McEachern, Stourhead and he exchange places, and would suggest that the transfer be made on 22nd February, by which time I expect the new men will be into the working of the Station.
>
> Robt. Muirhead
> Superintendent
> 15th January 1901[4]

Muirhead's primary concern, above all else, was that the light continued to work and Joseph Moore was therefore the best man for the job, at least until he (Muirhead) could find somebody suitable to replace him. Moore stayed on Eilean Mor until 9 March 1901, when he was transferred to Stourhead Lighthouse, no doubt much to Moore's relief, having served a total of one and a half years on the Flannan Isles.

With his investigations over and the presentation of his report dated 8 January 1900 to the NLB Commissioners, Muirhead then turned his attention to the problem of finding suitable long-term replacements for the Eilean Mor Lighthouse. There was also a pyschological barrier for the replacements to overcome, being sent to a remote station 20 miles out in the north-west Atlantic where three lightkeepers had vanished into thin air. However, the NLB lightkeepers collectively were hardy, professional men and carried out their work with stoicism.

Muirhead settled down and pored over the details of various keepers at all the stations to see which men were coming to the end of reasonable length tenures at their current stations and could be pulled in to the Flannan Isles at fairly short notice. Within a very short period of time, Muirhead decided on four men (three assistants and a principal) to transfer on a permanent (a standard period of duty on a single station) basis. Once again, however, fate would intervene for one of the replacements and the ill luck which surrounded the Flannan Islands in the early 1900s would see the Eilean Mor Lighthouse being the last posting for one of the men.

The first permanent replacement was Assistant Lightkeeper John McLachlan, who arrived on Eilean Mor on 29 January 1901. He was followed two days later on 31 January by Assistant Lightkeeper David Ross who was brought out by the lLighthouse tender *Hesperus.* One week later a third ALK, Angus McEachern, arrived on 7 February on the *Hesperus.* Finally, the last to arrive was William Beggs, a new principal to replace James Ducat, on 20 February. With all the replacements finally settled in, Robert Muirhead was at last able to allow Joseph Moore to leave the Flannan Islands on 9 March 1901, two and a half weeks after the arrival of new Principal William Beggs. Beggs was of the view that the missing lightkeepers were swept away whilst working on the crane that day and he devised a hook to be attached by rope to lightkeepers working on the crane to stop them being swept away by a wave. He sent the design to NLB headquarters.

While the tragedy played itself out in the news in early 1901, the three new ALKs (with one constantly acting as a rotating relief at the Breasclete shore station) and principal all settled down in their new station. Assistant Lightkeepers David Ross and Angus McEachern stayed on the Flannan Isles for just over five years and three years respectively. Principal William Beggs was to stay for four years and eight months before being transferred to Douglas Head. However, the first of the permanent ALKs to arrive on the Flannans, John McLachlan, was not so fortunate. When David Alan Stevenson designed the lighthouse on Eilean Mor, he decided that the height of the main island in the group dispensed with the need for the light tower on the Flannan Isles to be of a great height compared to, say, a light tower like the one on the Bell Rock, which was built at more or less sea level. The highest point on Eilean Mor was 280ft and although the light tower needed to rise above this and the surrounding islands of the Seven Hunters, Stevenson designed a light tower of which the optical apparatus was only 48ft above the 280ft height of Eilean Mor. Whilst a 50ft light tower was fairly short in lighthouse terms, it was a big enough drop to kill someone, particularly if they fell onto concrete. On 20 August 1904, three and a half years after he had arrived at the station, John McLachlan was working on the light tower when he slipped and fell to his death. It was tragic that the lighthouse on Eilean Mor had claimed the life of yet another NLB keeper within four years of the first tragedy. Nevertheless, McLachlan's death was viewed as just an unfortunate accident, which it was. Of the original arrivals after the tragedy on 15 December 1900, Assistant Lightkeeper David Ross and Principal William Beggs were still stationed on the Flannans at the time of McLachlan falling from the light tower. Angus McEachern had left three months earlier for Hyskeir on 18 May 1904. The sad death of McLachlan, coming not so long after the disappearances of Ducat, Marshall and Macarthur, must have had a sobering effect on both Ross and Beggs. Both men could have been forgiven for thinking that they had landed on a station cursed with such ill luck.

With the loss of men who died in the course of their work, the issue of gratuities and pensions inevitably arose. All of the keepers had families and other dependents who relied on the lightkeepers' salaries as their sole source of income. Superintendent Robert Muirhead took on the responsibility of attending to the dependents and families of the missing men, which cannot have been an enviable task.

James Ducat was the most senior with the longest service and also had the largest family. The second man in line of seniority on the Eilean Mor Lighthouse was Thomas Marshall. He was born on 11 April 1871 and had entered the service of the NLB as an ALK on 27 April 1896. At the time of his disappearance on 15 December 1900, he was twenty-nine years old and had been an ALK for four years and nine months.

On 15 December 1900, the third lightkeeper who should have been present on Eilean Mor was Assistant Lightkeeper William Ross. However, as he had been taken ill, he had been replaced by an Occasional Lightkeeper, Donald Macarthur. Macarthur, as stated previously, had only been in the service of the NLB for less than a year, having joined as an occasional on 29 January 1900 and undergone twenty-six nights' training from that date. Whilst Macarthur acted as OLK, his pay was at the rate of 5*s* per day and night with victualling, when he was present on the rock.

The situation regarding the dependents of Macarthur was somewhat different as he was an OLK rather than a full-time ALK. Mrs Macarthur's circumstances were poignantly put in a letter dated 14 January 1901.[5] It was written by William Ross, who knew the family well and for whom Donald Macarthur was covering while he was ill in Breasclete. The letter is addressed to the Secretary (James Murdoch) at NLB headquarters, 84 George Street, Edinburgh and reads:

Sir,
In reply to your letter of 10th Inst. requesting me to give all the information I can obtain about Mrs Macarthur widow of the late Occ & Keeper. I beg to say that Mrs Macarthur is 32 years of age with a family of two, a boy age 10, and a girl age 7 years, both at school. She came here 7 years ago with her late husband when he got his discharge from the Royal Engineers, afterwards being 5 years in the reserve. He was a native of Breascleit. She was born and brought up in Gravesend, England, and can get nothing to do here to earn a livelihood. If she had the means to pay her way she would go to her native place where she has friends and might get something to do for herself.

I am Sir
Your Most Obedient Servant
William Ross[6]

The circumstances under which payments of gratuities were made for deaths in service were already well laid out, and it is to the credit of the NLB that they tried to look beyond the cold hard facts to see the human element involved behind the tragedy, especially so in the case of Mrs Macarthur who was far away from her family and friends with two young children to support. The NLB accountant, William Boat, prepared a report on what payments and gratuities would be available to the dependants. The accountant acknowledges the strange circumstances in the first line of his report[7]:

> In consequence of the mysterious disappearance of the Lightkeepers on duty on the Flannan Islands lighthouse on or about 15 December 1900, the question of pension and gratuities, under the treasury warrant regulating the grant of Gratuities and Allowances under section I of the Superannuation Act 1887, comes up for consideration, regarding which I beg to report as follows[8]:

The accountant then goes on to list the men's details of their service with the NLB before stating what the strict entitlement would be under the terms of the 1887 Superannuation Act, which was basically to cover civil service workers who were killed in the line of their work. This came under Scale II of the Act which covered what was to be paid out to the widows and children of the deceased. The pension payable to the widows was not to exceed $^{10}/_{60}$ of their husband's salary and any emoluments, or £10 a year – whichever was greater.

The gratuity to the children of the deceased was not to exceed £1, multiplied by the total number of their years, starting from their ages at the time of their father's deaths and ending at fifteen years. The total gratuity payable was not to be less than £10 or more than £50 in each case.   Both James Ducat and Thomas Marshall came under these terms and allowances.

As principal lightkeeper, James Ducat received total pay and emoluments of £96 8s 9d of which $^{10}/_{60}$ gave Mrs Ducat a pension of £16 1s 6d. James Ducat left four children: Louisa (sixteen years), Robert (thirteen years), Annabella (nine years) and Arthur (six years). At sixteen years of age, his eldest child Louisa was unfortunately past the cut-off point to be considered for a gratuity, but under the terms of the Act the remaining children received a total of £17 between them, worked out as follows:

15 Years − 13 = 2 x £1 = £2
15 Years − 9 = 6 x £1 = £6
15 Years − 6 = 9 x £1 = £9

It is hard reading the cold facts on paper of how the money was apportioned. The statement for Louisa merely reads: 'Louisa is over age and does not count.'

The child had just lost her father in dreadful circumstances and received no form of compensation on account of being one year past the cut-off point. It could certainly be argued that the nature of the men's deaths on duty was such a highly unusual occurrence that there may have been some grounds for leniency in the rules. A yearly pension was payable to Mrs (Mary) Ducat from 1 January 1901 of 16 1s 6d plus a gratuity of £17 for the youngest children. The payment of her pension was as long as she remained 'unmarried' and of 'Good Character'.

Regarding leniency in the rules, there was initially some attempt at understanding and generosity in the case of Thomas Marshall. The twenty-nine-year-old Marshall was unmarried and it was only notified to the accountant during the preparation of his report that his mother had just died. He still had a father who was alive, along with a brother and sister. While the NLB awaited confirmation of Marshall's mother's death, the report stated the conditions laid out in the warrant (under the 1887 Superannuation Act) for an unmarried man at the time of his death: 'If the deceased does not leave a widow, and if his mother was wholly dependent upon him for her support, the award which might have been made to the widow may be made to the mother.'

It was felt that the regulations did not apply fully in Marshall's case, as the mother did not appear to have been dependent on her son. Had the regulations applied, Marshall had a service of less than five years with the NLB and a total pay and emoluments which amounted to £82 15s, which would have amounted to a gratuity of one half of Marshall's salary and emoluments being £41 7s 6d. The accountant then went on to recommend to the NLB Commissioners that, owing to the special circumstances of the Flannan Isles disaster, a suitable amount of gratuity could be paid to the representatives of Thomas Marshall (presumably his father, brother and sister as they were not specifically identified in the recommendation). In other words the accountant found that basically Marshall's surviving relatives were due to receive nothing as a Gratuity (apart from the life insurance policy payout), but that a special case should be considered for making a gesture to his relatives. The lack of further correspondence on this implies that nothing in the way of a gratuity was paid to the relatives of Thomas Marshall, because on 11 May 1901 a letter was sent by Mr David Brown, the Manager of the Maybole branch of the Royal Bank of Scotland to the NLB secretary.[9] The letter introduced the Bank Manager as an agent of Thomas Marshall's father, John Marshall of Seabank, Maidens. Mr Brown had stated that he had known John Marshall for many years and acted for him as an agent in the past. The letter stressed that John Marshall was seventy years old and was unable to continue his profession as a seaman as he was too old and had no other means of support. David Brown then said that although he felt there was a claim arising under statute and common law, he was making the approach to the NLB in a 'friendly spirit' (which he underlined). He said that based on Thomas Marshall's salary 'of at least £60' (actually underestimated by over £20) and three years of work, he wished to 'earnestly press' (again underlined) for a 'friendly reconsideration of his case' (which implies that a decision had already been made not to make a payment). Brown then goes on to say that he feels a gratuity one-off payment to John Marshall of £100 would be suitable under the circumstances. This appeal appears to have been rejected by the NLB because on 5 June 1901, a further letter[10] arrived from Brown addressed to C. Dick Peddie esq. (who had replaced

James Murdoch as NLB Secretary), referring to the NLB's letter dated 23 May 1901.[11] Brown says that he had met with John Marshall and did not wish to push their claim through legal means (and he mentions that he feels a legal case is justified) but that John Marshall wishes to pursue his case in a 'friendly' manner. The letter continues in this vein for half a page, again mentioning the support provided to his parents by Thomas Marshall and again stressing that John Marshall could not follow his former profession as a seafarer. It then finishes with a not too subtle threat:

> I should be very averse to bringing Mr Marshall's case under notice of Parliament; but, as I consider it a most claimant and distressing case, I may in the event of a satisfactory allowance not being conceded, be obliged, however reluctantly, to ask a Member of Parliament to take up the matter in the House of Commons and elsewhere.[12]

The letter finishes with the hope that the NLB will see their way clear to considering the full payment of £100 as originally suggested by him (David Brown). There is a postscript which stresses the severe trial that John Marshall has had with both the death of his son and wife close together and that he 'deserves kind treatment'. It was a not unreasonable point to make under the circumstances. John Marshall had stated himself in a letter to the NLB on 22 February 1901[13] that his daughter was in employment as an acting sub post mistress of the Post Office in Maybole and was waiting for the Post Office to decide if she should be made permanent sub post mistress, so his daughter was in gainful employment at this time. Despite the unsubtle threat made in the letter from David Brown asking a member of parliament to take up John Marshall's case, the NLB appear to have been unperturbed and C. Dick Peddie responded to David Brown in a letter on 14 June 1901 stating:

Dear Sir,

I am directed to inform you that the Commissioners, after careful consideration, regret that they cannot accede to your claim on behalf of Mr John Marshall. Your statement – in answer to a request for detailed information – that Mr Marshall is without means and that his son was in the habit of remitting him considerable sums for his support, is of too general a nature to be of much weight. It is, further, apparently inconsistent with information supplied to the Commissioners shortly after the accident by Mr Marshall senior himself, to the effect that at the time of his son's death he was still pursuing his calling as Master of a coasting vessel, and that any pecuniary assistance afforded by his son to members of the family had consisted of occasional gifts of money to his sister.

In view of these statements and of Mr Marshall's declared intention of living with his daughter, the Commissioners divided between them the proceeds of a policy of insurance for £140 on the son's life; had Mr Marshall been considered entitled to a gratuity or annuity a different disposition of the money would have been made.

I may add that the Commissioners understand that Mr Marshall also derives considerable benefit from the proceeds of another policy of insurance taken out by his son.

The case is not provided for in the Superannuation Acts and relative Treasury Warrants by which the Commissioners' action in such matters is regulated, and the Commissioners, while sympathising with Mr Marshall in his bereavement, regret that the circumstances so far as disclosed to them do not warrant them in recommending that an action be made in respect of his claim.

Yours Faithfully
(Sgd) C. Dick Peddie
Secretary[14]

That then appears to have been the end of the matter as far as the NLB was concerned and presumably it was an end of the matter for John Marshall and his agent David Brown, as no further correspondence appears to have been forthcoming. Whilst it appears on the face of it that John Marshall had perhaps overstated his case and there were implied threats of 'going public' though a member of parliament, one cannot blame him for trying to get what he could under the circumstances. His son was still a relatively young man with plenty of working life ahead of him and had died during the course of his work.

Coming to the case of Mrs Macarthur and her two children, again the accountant showed an understanding of the plight she was in and he pressed the Commissioners to be magnanimous towards her and the children. The report stated that Donald Macarthur's circumstances came under Scale III in the warrant which was: 'Any other hired person employed in a public department.'[15]

There was a reservation to any award, however, as the regulations stated that if the service of the deceased was less than five years at the date of death/injury, any award to a widow would take the form of a gratuity not exceeding one half of a year's salary and emoluments. Macarthur had actually been employed for less than a year and his widow was therefore still eligible to receive one half of the salary he had earned up to the date of his death - amounting to £26 10s 5d. One positive point in the warrant was that although he had been employed as an OLK for barely a year, Macarthur's two children were both eligible for a gratuity not exceeding one twelfth of his salary and emoluments, although this was capped by the total to Mrs Macarthur and the two children not receiving in total more than one year's salary and emoluments that Macarthur would have received. The gratuity to the two children amounted to £4 8s 5d each making a total of £35 7s 3d including the sum paid to Mrs Macarthur. The accountant, in writing his report, appealed to the Commissioners to consider making a larger payment to Mrs Macarthur and her children.[16] To support his argument, he first mentioned the case of a seaman named Will who had died in an accident on the crane at Sule Skerry for which his mother was awarded a gratuity of £125. Then he brought up the case of two boys at Pretoria Day at Lossiemouth, one of whom had been killed and the other seriously injured. In these cases the Commissioners had agreed that gratuities be paid of £20 and £30 respectively. He stated that the total gratuity being offered to Mrs Macarthur seemed to be a very inadequate sum as recognition for the loss of her husband and, in his position as accountant, recommended that the Commissioners request the sanction of the Board of Trade for a gratuity to Mrs Macarthur of not less than £100 plus the recommendation of a payment of an annual pension of £10. It was a decent gesture which recognised the special circumstances of the Flannans disaster and it would have been a good outcome for Mrs Macarthur and her children, considering her late husband's short time with the NLB. In the event, however, the Board of Trade, who gave the ultimate sanction for the payments returned Mrs Macarthur's marriage certificate and children's birth certificates on 18 March 1901 to the NLB with a letter stating they did not agree to the pension proposal and would only sanction a payment to her of £50 plus £20 for both children. This was £30 less than the NLB proposal but was almost double what the official entitlement would have been, so it was still not a bad outcome for the family.

The accountant's report then went on to give details of the sums and policies for James Ducat and Thomas Marshall. Both men's lives had been insured with the North British and Mercantile Insurance Company. Finally, in another gesture of great decency, the accountant stated that none of the wages and allowances for the three men had been paid since their disappearance and he recommended that even though they had disappeared on or around 15 December, their wages and allowances should be paid up to the end of the quarter (i.e. the end of December 1900) and that sanction should be sought from the Board of Trade to allow this payment to the men's families or their representatives. The Board of Trade agreed to the proposal that the three missing lightkeepers have their wages paid in full up until 31 December 1900.

As well as the report for the Commissioners concerning payments to the families, the accountant, William Boat, prepared a further memorandum for the Commissioners regarding Mrs Ducat, suggesting that, although it would involve extra administrative work, payments to Mrs Ducat should be made by the offices at 84 George Street upon her application when she felt she needed money. It was felt this arrangement would help her better as she was left alone to bring up four children, two of whom were under the age of ten years. Once again it was a small gesture of decency from William Boat.

In 1901, deliberations over money and costs also concerned the NLB on the subject of the building work for the lighthouse on Eilean Mor. Despite the lighthouse becoming operational on 7 December 1899, building work had been ongoing, even though the bulk of it had been completed. The work was officially finished in October 1900. However there were serious arguments about costs and payments with the contractor (*see below*).

The wider world had also become acquainted with the tragedy through the newspapers. After the telegram had been sent by Captain Harvey of the *Hesperus* to James Murdoch, the NLB Secretary, informing them of the missing lightkeepers, the news rapidly spread, with the first reports in newspapers appearing on Friday 28 December 1900. Virtually every newspaper in the country reported on the tragedy in one form or another over the following weeks. These included such newspapers as the *Aberdeen Journal, Oban Times, Oban Express, Arbroath Herald and Advertiser for the Montrose Burghs, Inverness Courier*, as well as in England with papers as regionally diverse as the *Hull Daily Mail, Bath Weekly Chronicle and Gazette* and the *Leicester Chronicle*.

Aftermath

The newspaper which probably gave the most comprehensive overview of the events was the *Scotsman* through their Stornoway correspondent. On 28 December 1900, two days after the arrival of the *Hesperus* at Eilean Mor, an article entitled 'Disaster at a Lewis Lighthouse - Three Men Drowned' appeared:

A telegram was received yesterday morning from Callernish, Island of Lewis, by the Northern Lighthouse Commissioners, stating that disaster had overtaken the three lighthouse keepers on the Flannan Islands. This group of rocky islets lies off the mouth of Loch Roag. They are seven in number and are sometimes called 'The Seven Hunters.' On the largest of them – Eilean Mor, as it is called – the Northern Lighthouse Commissioners erected a lighthouse, which was first lighted on the 7th December 1899. Designed by the Messrs D. & C. Stevenson, CE, Edinburgh, the Commissioners engineers, it took four seasons to build, partly on account of the stormy waters around it, and also from the difficulty there was in landing stones and material.

This island, which is egg shaped, has cliffs all round of not less than 150 feet in height. Above the cliff line there is a steep grassy band facing the south, which carries the land of the island to a height of over 200 feet. On the north side the cliffs have a straight descent to the sea. The lighthouse was erected on the highest land, and was a stone structure fitted to resist the gales which blow in wildly from the Atlantic. There is no land between the Flannan Islands and America. The tower of the lighthouse rises 75 feet above the island, and the light, which is of 140,000 candle power, could be seen for 24 nautical miles. The chief purpose it served was to give a lead and direction to vessels going from the Atlantic by the Butt of Lewis to the Pentland Firth, or coming from the Firth to the Great Western Ocean. The Commissioners made two landing places, one at the east side and the other at the west, to be used according to the way the wind was blowing. From these they had to cut a zig-zag stair up the face of the cliffs to the grassy slope already referred to. And they also constructed a trolley tramway, worked from the lighthouse by an engine and rope, for the purpose of taking stores from the landing stages to the lighthouse.

At each of the landing stages but higher up the cliff, is a crane for unloading stores from the Commissioners' steamers. There are, it may be further explained, four lighthouse men attached to this station. Three of them are always on the rock attending to the light. Each of the four in turn is six weeks on the island, and a fortnight on the mainland. During that fortnight they reside at the town of Breasclete, on the north side of Loch Roag where the Commissioners have built substantial cottages for their staff, their wives and families, or other relations. The Flannans are visited every fortnight by the Commissioners' steamer *Hesperus*; and it was on this vessel, which is under the command of Captain Harvey, making her usual call at the lighthouse with stores on Wednesday, that the unfortunate discovery was made that the whole of the lighthouse staff were missing. But for the lighthouse men these rocky and lonely islands are uninhabited. The *Hesperus* left Oban on Monday, and took on board the keeper, who after his fortnight on shore, was returning to relieve one of his comrades. On the boat's crew landing at Eilean Mohr no one was to be seen. The tower and the residences of the keepers were searched, but none of the men could be found. A rocket was fired, but there was no response, and the painful conviction was forced home: that the lighthouse keepers had been swept off the island and drowned.

All the clocks in the building were stopped, from which it is considered possible that the disaster occurred at least a week ago – presumably on Thursday last, the 20th – the day of the terrible gale which did so much damage all over Scotland, and wrecked part of the Shetland fishing fleet. How the disaster occurred to the lighthouse men is only as yet matter of conjecture. When the first intimation of it arrived in Edinburgh it could only be guessed that they had been blown over the cliffs, as nothing was said about any damage to the lighthouse itself. What they were doing outside in such a gale could not be conjectured. The names of the men missing are James Ducat, principal keeper, who is married and has a family of four; Thomas Marshall, unmarried; and an occasional keeper, Donald Mc'Arthur [sic], who is married, and had temporarily taken the place of one of the regular keepers who is ill on shore. The relief keeper whose name is More, and three of the crew of the *Hesperus* were left on the island to attend to the light, while the vessel returned to anchorage for the night to Loch Roag. Yesterday the *Hesperus* again made for the Flannans, but a telegram which was received in Edinburgh in the course of the day stated that the sea was too rough for landing to be effected at either of the stages. Captain Harvey, however, got into signal communication with the men on the island, and learned that one of the cranes already referred to on the cliff had been destroyed; and it is now thought that the unfortunate men may have ventured out of the lighthouse in the gale; in order to try and save the crane, and been washed away. Something more may be known of the circumstances of the disaster when Captain Harvey is able to land on the island, and another attempt will be made to do so today. It seems that at Breasclete on the mainland, there is a lookout station, from which the Flannan lighthouse can be seen. The signalman there, seeing no adverse signal from the lighthouse, apprehended nothing wrong, though he did not see the light for these last few nights past. That he attributed to the thickness of the atmosphere. This, it seems, is quite an unprecedented calamity in the history of the Northern Lighthouse Commission. The last disaster was nearly fifty years ago; when an attending boat, running between Kirkcudbright and the Little Ross lighthouse, was lost with all hands.

Telegraphing last night, our Stornoway correspondent states that during the day information of the disaster was received there, though nothing definite beyond the fact that the three lighthouse keepers had lost their lives was known. The people of that part of the Lewis which is nearest to the Flannan Islands, he adds, were alarmed when for two or three nights past they could see no trace of the Flannan light – a fact which was communicated by telegraph to the Lighthouse Commissioners.

The Flannan or 'Flannel Isles' as they are called in the Statistical Account of Scotland, are rather interesting rocky islets, and are supposed to have been the residency of eccclisiastics in the time of the Druids. They are called by Buchanan Insule Sacre. There is at least one ruin on Eilean Mohr of some small ecclesiastical building – known as 'the Blessing Chapel' – just below the spot on which the lighthouse is now erected. The islands, which are attached to the parish of Uig, are, as has already been stated, a rocky cluster, seven in number, with narrow waterways between them. The total area they cover would be about two miles by a quarter of a mile, the long way being east and west. The largest of the group, Eilean Mohr [sic], is barely a quarter of a mile across. The cliffs are of gneiss. Nearly all the members of the group have this in common that their sides are precipitous. Formerly, a few sheep belonging to people on the mainland were grazed on the islands, but that has been given up for many years. M'Culloch speaks of the islands of being a great resort for sea birds but people who lately visited them say that in that respect there is nothing very remarkable about them. In connection with what has been said as to the association of the Druids with this lovely group of rocky islands, it may be recalled that at Callernish, near the head of Loch Roag, are the celebrated Druidical standing stones – forming one of the most complete remains of the kind in the Kingdom, while at the neighbouring township of Carloway is one of the largest and most perfect Danish forts or domes to be met in Scotland. It was on the sands of the bay of Uig in 1831 that a number of small Ivory sculptured figures, resembling chessmen, were found, and being of great antiquity, were transferred to the Antiquarian Society of Edinburgh.[17]

The *Scotsman*'s account then continues under the heading 'An Old Account of the Flannan Islands' which is taken from Martin Martin's writings:

In Martin Martin's volume 'A Description of the Western Isles of Scotland' dated 1695, a chapter is devoted to 'Inferior Islands' adjacent to Lewis. Dealing with the subject the writer says:

Near to the north-west promontory of Carlway Bay, called Gallan-Head, are the little islands of Pabbay, Shirem, Vaxay, Wuya the Great and Lesser. To the north-west of Gallan-Head, and within six league of it, lie the Flannan Islands, which the seamen call North Hunters; they are but small islands and six in number, and maintain about seventy sheep yearly. The inhabitants of the adjacent lands of the Lewis, having a right to these islands, visit them once every summer, and there make a great purchase of fowls, eggs, down, feathers, and quills. When they go to sea they have their boat well manned, and make forwards the islands with an east wind; but if before or at the landing the wind turn westerly they hoist up sail and steer directly home again. If any of their crew is a novice and not versed in the customs of the place, he must be instructed perfectly in all the punctilloes observed here before landing, and to prevent inconvenience that they think may ensue upon the transgression of the least nicety observed here, every novice is always joined with another that can instruct him all the time of their fowling; so all the boats crew are matched in this manner. After their landing they fasten the boat to the sides of a rock then fix a wooden ladder by laying a stone at the foot of it to prevent its falling into the sea, and when they are got up into the island all of them uncover their heads and make a turn sun-ways round, thanking God for their safety.

The biggest of these islands is called Island-More; it has the ruins of a chapel dedicated to Saint Flannan from whom the island derives its name. When they are come within about twenty paces of the altar they all strip themselves of their upper garments at once, and their upper clothes being laid upon a stone, which stands there on purpose for that use, all the crew pray three times before they begin fowling; the first day they say the first prayer, advancing towards the chapel upon their knees; the second prayer is said as they go round the chapel; the third is said hard by or at the chapel; and this is their morning service. Their vespers are performed with the like number of prayers. Another rule is that it is absolutely unlawful to kill a fowl with a stone, for that they reckon a great barbarity and directly contrary to ancient custom.

It is also unlawful to kill a fowl before the ascend by the ladder. It is absolutely unlawful to call the island of St Kilda (which lies thirty leagues southward) by its proper Irish name, Hirt, but only the high country. They must not so much as once name the islands in which they are fowling by the ordinary name Flannan, but only the country. There are several other things that must not be called by their common names – e.g. Visk, which in the language of the natives signifies water, they call Burn; a Rock which in their language is Crag, must here be called Cruey – which is hard; Shore in their language expressed by Claddach, must here be called Vah – i.e. a Cave; Sour in their language is expressed by Gort, but here must be called Gaire – i.e. Sharp; Slippery, which is expressed Bog, must be called Soft; and several other things to this purpose. They count it also unlawful to kill a fowl after evening prayers. There is an ancient custom by which the crew not to carry home any sheep suet. Let them kill ever so many sheep in these islands.

One of their principal customs is not to steal or eat anything unknown to their partner, else the transgressor (they say) will certainly vomit it up, which they reckon as a just judgement. When they have loaded their boat sufficiently with sheep, fowl, eggs, down, fish, etc., they make the best of their way home. It is observed of the sheep of these islands that they are exceedingly fat and have long horns.

I had this superstitious account not only from several natives of the Lewis, but likewise from two who had been in the Flannan Islands the preceding year. I asked one of them if he prayed at home as often and as frequently as he did in the Flannan Islands, and he plainly confessed to me that he did not, adding, further, that these remote islands were places of inherent sanctity, and that there was none ever yet landed in them but found himself more disposed to there than anywhere else. The Island of Pigmies – or, as the natives call it, the Island of Little Men – is but of small extent. There has been many small bone dug out of the ground here, resembling those of human kind more than any other. This gave ground to a tradition which the natives have of a very low-statured people, living once here, called Losbirdan – i.e. Pigmies.[18]

In response to this lengthy article regarding the disaster and the Flannan Isles, the following day a letter was published in the same paper from the NLB Secretary James Murdoch. He was quick to point out an error in the article:

Sir

In the account in today's 'Scotsman' of the lamentable disaster to the lighthouse keepers, on the Flannan Islands, it is stated, on the authority of your Stornoway correspondent, that 'The people of that part of the Lewis which is nearest to the Flannan Islands were alarmed when for two or three nights past they could see no trace of the Flannan light – a fact which was communicated by telegraph to the Lighthouse Commissioners.'

I shall be obliged by your correcting this statement. The news of the disaster was telegraphed to the Commissioners on the evening of the 26th inst. by the master of their steamer 'Hesperus.' Prior to that date the Commissioners had received no communication of any kind relating to the Flannan Island Lighthouse or lighthouse keepers since the last relief was effected on the 7th inst., when all was well.

I may add that, owing to the distance of the lighthouse and the prevalence of haze at this season of year, there would be nothing remarkable in the light not being observed from the mainland for several nights in succession.

I am etc.
James Murdoch
Scy.[19]

Another article[20] in the *Scotsman* on the same day that James Murdoch's correction was printed related to a visit made in April 1900, to the lighthouse on the Flannan Islands by a minister of the Church. He describes his trip out to the lighthouse in the *Hesperus* and being shown around by James Ducat who returned to Breasclete with him in the *Hesperus*. Ducat had returned to Breasclete with the minister for his leave ashore. In a poignant note which was similar to the comment made at the end of Muirhead's report about the men's fate, the minister wrote:

> We took Ducat off with us that afternoon as it was his turn ashore, and I last saw him the same evening, as I can see him now, at the gate of his house, glad to be once more at home with wife and children. He was a most civil and pleasant man, and I little thought there was such a tragedy in store for him and his brave comrades on outpost duty.[21]

He finished his article with a description of the *Hesperus* making her way back to Oban from Breasclete ending with: 'Alas! There will always now be a sadness connected with thoughts of the Flannan Islands and their first lighthouse keepers.'[22]

It was almost inevitable in the aftermath of the disaster that attention would immediately focus on the signalling and why it apparently had not been noticed that there was no operational light for at least eleven days. It could have been expected that some sort of blame may have attached itself to gamekeeper Roderick MacKenzie, but this was not the case. On 9 July 1901, Robert Muirhead wrote a report for the Lighthouse Commissioners regarding signalling arrangements. In the report he stated that from February to November 1900, no assistance of any kind had been required as no signals had been exhibited by the lightkeepers on Eilean Mor. It was therefore difficult to tell, owing to the visibility, that had a signal been shown whether it would have been seen by Roderick Mackenzie or his sons. Mackenzie had been instructed to keep a record of which days he could see the tower and the light and which days both could not be seen (*see* Appendix II). Muirhead stated that the tower had been seen on 146 days and not seen on 219 days and that he was of the opinion that if the signals had been put up on any of the days that the tower could be seen, then the signals would most likely have been observable. He made the very good point that after the disaster there was nobody left to put up any kind of a signal, and that it was not until the *Hesperus* arrived that anybody realised anything was wrong. Muirhead wished to be seen to give Mackenzie the benefit of any doubt and stated: 'I am of opinion that the present system of signalling has not as yet been fairly and properly tested.'[23]

Muirhead then went on to suggest that Mackenzie be employed for a further twelve months and that the lightkeepers should put up the signal 'Send Boat' two days before the relief was due to be made. This was so that even if the signal could not be seen, the NLB would be aware that a signal was present, even if the observers could not see it. From this the NLB could work out how often the light was not visible due to the haze over the island and thereby judge properly how efficient the system was. Muirhead was not going to inform Mackenzie that the signal was being shown so as not to forewarn him, to allow a fairer test of the system. Once Mackenzie had seen the signal of his own accord, the new system and why it was being done that way, it would give him a better understanding of the new procedure. Muirhead did not feel that it was being particularly unfair to Mackenzie either, as basically what the signal was requesting was for the vessel to come out just before its appointed time, bringing the relief keeper and returning the other keeper to shore for his leave.

It was perhaps inevitable that the difficulties inherent in manual signalling pushed the NLB into having the Flannans become a wireless signalling station operated by Lloyds. An agreement was reached on the terms for such a station in November 1901 and approved by the Commissioners in December 1901. It is doubtful whether the presence of signalling/telegraph equipment would have made any difference to what happened on the 15 December 1900 but at least with better communications, the sinificance of a lack of communication may have meant that the disaster may have been noted sooner.

The other issue that was occuring before, during and after the disaster in December was the problem of the NLB reaching an accommodation over final payment to the contractor, George Lawson of Glasgow, for the building work on the station on Eilean Mor and the shore station at Breasclete. Although work finished in October 1900, ten months after the lighthouse became operational, the nature of the work and the difficulties of bringing materials and men out to the island had led George Lawson to make a serious underestimate in the calculations on which he based his estimate for the tender which that him the contract for building the station. On the day that Muirhead produced his report on the disaster (8 January 1901), David Alan Stevenson was also writing a memo[24] for the Commissioners in which he stated that out of a total sum of £14,889 11s Lawson was asking for consideration of the sum of £2,517 1s 8d (a sum adjusted by Stevenson from the total requested by Lawson of £4,085 11s). Amongst other miscalculations, Lawson had seriously underestimated the freight for carrying materials out to the island. He had allowed a total of £300 against an eventual cost of £1,740 for the four seasons. Another error made in tendering by Lawson was his assumption that fresh water, sand and stone would be available for the building work on the island. This was after his first visit there in May 1896, but in the event, he had to arrange to carry all these items over from Lewis, thereby massively increasing the cost and time taken. Masons had had to be brought from hard stone districts including Aberdeen and Peebles, with their passages paid both ways. Stevenson stated that the miscalculations were understandable as the Flannan Isles work was the most difficult undertaken of all the stations so far and he felt that calculating such costs was extremely difficult, recommending that the Commissioners at least have a meeting with Lawson to hear him put his case. Despite the Commissioners looking to make a part payment of £1,000 to Lawson in recognition of his loss, when put to the Board of Trade for approval it was rejected on the grounds that it was unfair to other companies who had tendered in good faith.

After the sea hitting and washing away the cranes in December 1900 and the close potential accident with Thomas Marshall in April 1900, problems with the crane on the west landing continued into 1901. What was described as a rough trip was made on the NLB Tender *Pharos* from Loch Roag out to the Flannans on 2 August 1901 by the Lighthouse Commissioners (on an inspection voyage). It was the first such trip that the Commissioners had made to the Flannans since the lighthouse started operations. They had just inspected the shore station at Breasclete and despite the rough crossing from Lewis, they made a fairly smooth landing. the inspection taking place only around seven months after the disaster, the disappearance of the lightkeepers must have weighed heavily on their minds as they set foot on Eilean Mor. Their report[25] found everything in order after a tour of the station, but they noted, with regret, a recent accident to the crane at the west landing. A defective cog had caused the butt end of the 50ft jib to snap and fall to the landing area 70ft below, fortunately with no injury to either the lightkeepers or crew members of a boat moored underneath the crane at the time. No mention was made of the loss of Ducat, Marshall or Macarthur in the report of the visit.[26]

As a postscript to the saga, Superintendent Robert Muirhead had investigated the disappearances while he was in his early forties. He had joined the NLB as an assistant superintendent in 1881 before being promoted to chief superintendent in 1884. The job of superintendent, it was felt, required men of character and fortitude; surprisingly, Muirhead was a man who was always considered to have been of 'delicate health'. In addition to what can only have been a stressful job as superintendent for the NLB, Muirhead was very civic-minded and as a native of Edinburgh (he lived at Broomieknowe, Lasswade) was elected to Bonnyrigg Town Council in 1902. He became senior bailie three years later. In 1913 his health required him to step down from his duties. After a period of rest he was able to take up his duties with the NLB once again. He continued until the very end of December 1915 when ill health again forced him to stop working. Three weeks later he passed away at the relatively early age of fifty-eight. A stressful job which required constant travel to the remote areas of the Scottish coast and islands as well as the Isle of Man cannot have helped his health. There is also no doubt that the disappearance of Ducat, Marshall and Macarthur could not have failed to have affected him, as he was the last person to see them alive and shake their hands as he said goodbye when he left them on Eilean Mor on 7 December 1900, eight days before.

Notes

1 Telegram copies, Scottish National Archives file no. NLC3/1/1.
2 Ibid.
3 Extract of report by Superintendent Robert Muirhead, 8 January 1901, Scottish National Archives file no. NLC3/1/1.
4 Memo by Superintendent Robert Muirhead, 15 January 1901, Scottish National Archives file no. NLC3/1/1.
5 Letter from William Ross regarding family of Donald Macarthur, 14 January 1901, Scottish National Archives file no. NLC3/1/1.
6 Ibid.
7 Report by NLB accountant on pension and annuity payments, February 1901, Scottish National Archives file nos NLC3/1/1, NLC2/1/88' NLC2/1/89.
8 Ibid.
9 Letter from David Brown to NLB secretary, 11 May 1901, Scottish National Archives file no. NLC3/1/1.
10 Letter from David Brown to NLB secretary, 5 June 1901, Scottish National Archives file no. NLC3/1/1.
11 This letter is referred to in David Brown's letter, but there is no copy in the Scottish National Archives.
12 Letter from David Brown to NLB secretary, 5 June 1901, Scottish National Archives file no. NLC3/1/1.
13 Letter from John Marshall to the NLB, 22 February 1901, Scottish National Archives file no. NLC3/1/1.
14 Letter from NLB secretary to David Brown, 14 June 1901, Scottish National Archives file no. NLC3/1/1.
15 Report by NLB accountant on pension and annuity payments, February 1901, Scottish National Archives file nos NLC3/1/1, NLC2/1/88, NLC2/1/89.
16 Ibid.
17 'Disaster at a Lewis Lighthouse – Three Men Drowned', article in *Scotsman* newspaper, 28 December 1900.
18 Ibid.
19 Letter from NLB secretary in *Scotsman*, 29 December 1900.
20 Article in *Scotsman*, 29 December 1900.
21 Ibid.
22 Ibid.

23 Report on signalling by Robert Muirhead, 9 July 1901, Scottish National Archives file no. NLC3/1/1.
24 Memo from David Alan Stevenson to NLB Commissioners, 8 January 1900, Scottish National Archives file no. NLC3/1/1.
25 Report on visit by NLB Commissioners to the Flannans, 2 August 1901, Scottish National Archives file no. NLC3/1/1.
26 Ibid.

GIANT WAVE[1]

Before considering the giant wave theory, one possibility considered by NLB Superintendent Robert Muirhead is that the three men were possibly on the cliff edge at the top of the West landing and all three were blown off the cliffs and down into the sea by the strong wind. He stated in his report:

> I have considered and discussed the possibility of the men being blown away by the wind, but, as the wind was westerly, I am of opinion, notwithstanding its great force, that the more probable explanation is that they have been washed away, as, had the wind caught them, it would, from its direction, have blown them up the island, and I feel certain that they would have managed to throw themselves down before they reached the summit or brow of the island.[2]

This supposition, of course, assumes that the men were only at the west landing and ignoring the ruling that at least one of them should have been inside the light station at all times and, again, it also assumes that Macarthur was with Ducat and Marshall in his shirtsleeves. Would there have been any reason for them to have gone to the west landing considering there appears little point in them doing so? Would it also have been a possibility that the three may have been on another cliff edge on Eilean Mor exposed to the wind with the danger of being blown off and into the sea? As it was daylight, is it possible that one of them had seen what he thought to be a boat in trouble close to the island, and that the three of them had rushed to a cliff edge for a better look? This again is unlikely, as there were no reported ships or smaller boats in the area, notwithstanding the violent gale that was blowing. Even allowing for the fact that the three men had been cooped up in the light station itself for several days on account of the weather, it seems again to be a highly unlikely scenario that they would have gone outside for a break from the monotony of being cooped up inside the tiny station, given the conditions. By the nature of their job, lighthousemen were used to being cooped up in tower lighthouses for days and weeks on end. It was the very essence of the job. Barring any other possibility that the three of them had cause to go out to another location on Eilean Mor (with Macarthur in his shirtsleeves) for some reason, being blown into the sea by the wind can probably be ruled out.

To the casual observer skimming over the facts, the three men went down to the west landing where a giant wave came and before the men had time to scramble to safety, the wave hit the west landing and the force of water which went above them then swept down and washed them all into the sea and they drowned there.

Bearing in mind the fact that there is little doubt among many theorists the three lightkeepers were swept away by a giant wave, one of the most pertinent questions is why did all three of them put themselves in such a position in the first place? The weather was bad on Saturday 15 December 1900. Contemporary weather reports for 2 p.m. that day (around the time the men disappeared) showed wind and sea to be Force 8 on the Beaufort Scale. On the previous evening the wind and sea was recorded as Force 4. At 8 a.m. the following morning the wind and sea had been recorded at Force 7, so the weather had worsened considerably and in the space of six hours from

8 a.m. to 2 p.m. it had got worse still, reaching Force 8. By 6 p.m. that day the weather had worsened yet again to Force 9 and was one stage below storm force, although the men were believed to have disappeared that afternoon.[3] On the face of it, after they had eaten lunch, Thomas Marshall and James Ducat went out into high westerly winds, a very heavy swell with waves over 30ft and more than likely, rain and large quantities of sea spray. Both Joseph Moore and Robert Muirhead mention in their reports that James Ducat was wearing sea boots and a waterproof and Thomas Marshall was wearing sea boots and oilskins. Muirhead draws the conclusion that they wore these items of weatherproof clothing to make their way down to the landing or somewhere near it. The main point Muirhead makes is that they left the station (lighthouse) itself to venture outside in appalling weather. Donald Macarthur is presumed to have also left the shelter of the lighthouse to go outside as well, but appears to have done so in his shirtsleeves. This assumption was made by Joseph Moore in his report but was not mentioned in Muirhead's report. Nonetheless, it can be assumed that Muirhead agreed with Moore's conclusion.

It is noteworthy that the crane, which was 70ft above the waterline, appeared to be undamaged. In any event, whilst damage to the crane could not be avoided owing to its fixed position, the box of ropes was another issue, as it could be argued that the three men on the station were aware of the potential of the effects of the sea on the west landing and any damage or loss to equipment there could be construed as negligence on their part with accompanying disciplinary measures, including fines, against them.

An argument could also be made as to why the west landing should be constantly in use when the eastern landing did not have such adverse weather conditions affecting it as often. Equally another argument could have been made as to why the box of ropes should be left on the west landing side and be constantly exposed to such terrible effects from the weather and sea with the potential for it to be washed away. However, lifting a large, heavy box of ropes backwards and forwards from a place of relative safety, say up by the station itself (i.e. the lighthouse building) would be a relatively pointless and tiresome task requiring two men and would also probably highlight a lack of confidence in the ability of the men to properly secure the box of ropes and any other equipment down on the west landing.

One odd item is that in Muirhead's report there is no mention of the storm damage seen by Muirhead in the station log itself. If the damage was mentioned in the log then Muirhead, for whatever reason, does not mention it. One would have expected him to do so if only to pinpoint the date the giant wave had hit the west landing. It is inconceivable that the men on the station would not have entered the damage in the log because not to have done so would have implied a lack of diligence on their part at the very least. Even if there was damage or loss of property, the railings which had been torn out of the concrete would have been impossible to repair on their own and would have required help from headquarters to arrange to send out men and materials to repair the damage. Possibly one main conclusion that can be drawn from this is that the damage caused by the giant wave happened after the men disappeared. The wind and the sea between 20 and 21 December 1900 was extreme enough for many reports to talk of storms and hurricanes in the newspapers. The very high winds which were blowing from the south-west across the Flannans increased in strength as they travelled further north and shifted to the north-west and four fishing trawlers were sunk in the Shetlands with the loss of twenty-two lives on 21 December in what came to be as known as the Delting Disaster.

Quite apart from Ducat's and Marshall's years of experience as lightkeepers, the idea that because the three lightkeepers were fairly new to the Flannan Islands and were not aware of the potential for giant waves to hit the west landing can be laid to rest with what happened shortly after the lighthouse became operational in December 1899. Originally, at the opening of the light station on Eilean Mor, there was not one but two cranes at the west landing. One crane was placed on the platform 70ft above sea level, and a second crane was a further 50ft above this one. This second crane was therefore 110ft above sea level at the top of the cliff edge. Before the end of December 1899, a giant wave had hit the west landing with enough power to wash away not just the lower crane, but also the higher crane at 110ft.[4] This had meant that the wave which hit the cranes must have had tremendous power and size which was enough to clear the cliff at the very top and drag anything down with it. The crane on the 70ft platform was replaced, but not the higher one. In addition to the cranes, two 25cwt Greenheart logs (of South American origin and used for their anti-rotting properties in marine environments), which had been stored in a crevice at 75ft, had also been completely swept away by the sea.[5] Whilst Donald Macarthur did not commence his duties with the NLB on the Flannans until the end of following month (January 1900), he would have been aware of the loss of the cranes and logs due to the wave. James Ducat and Thomas Marshall would have both been fully aware of the potential for a wave to clear the top of the cliff at the west landing which makes their behaviour all the more inexplicable if they did venture down there on the afternoon of 15 December 1900 when the wind and sea were increasing from Force 8 to Force 9 directly onto the landing.

One of the main questions also to be asked is why would any of the three lightkeepers even venture out in the foulest of weather, let alone down to the west landing with the potential danger there from large waves? The most likely answer to this question lies in the correspondence between the NLB headquarters in Edinburgh and James Ducat in his position as PLK on Eilean Mor, over eight months before the tragedy. Prior to this correspondence between James Ducat and 84 George Street, an official circular was sent out to all stations on 18 February 1898. The circular referred to an accident at Sule Skerry. On 5 April 1900, a letter[6] was sent to James Ducat in his position as principal lighthouse keeper on the Flannan Isles. The letter was written by James Murdoch, the NLB secretary, and was in response to a letter he had received from Ducat on 24 February 1900 concerning a minor accident involving the crane on the west landing at the Flannan Isles Station. Murdoch's letter to Ducat stated:

Sir,

Referring to your letter of 24th February last, reporting the accident to the crane, while under manipulation by Mr Marshall, one of your Assistants, I am to call your attention prominently to the circular which was issued on 18th February 1898, (of the contents of which both you and Mr Marshall are aware, and of which I enclose a copy), holding you responsible for seeing that the crane, hoisting gear, etc., are kept in a sound and efficient state and are in every respect reliable etc., etc. This circular is sufficient to impress on you the absolute necessity of exerting the utmost care and attention in the use of the crane, and it would appear that, on the recent occasion, there must have been thoughtlessness, at least on Mr Marshall's part, or the accident would not have happened.

Fortunately no one was hurt, but, as there might have been very serious consequences, I have to impress upon you and the other Keepers at the Station, to whom you will read this letter, not only to bestow such care on the crane and its machinery and tackle as is necessary to keep it efficient, but also to be very careful in the handling of it. The foregoing remarks also apply to the landing derricks.

Your Obedient Servant,
James Murdoch,
Secretary[7]

It is a 'no-nonsense' letter and despite signing himself as 'Obedient Servant' (the style of the time), it is clearly written from a superior to his subordinate and it is written in a style which brooks no further discussion or dissent on the matter. Whilst accidents happen, it is clear from the tone of this letter that James Murdoch was not interested in listening to any excuses. There had been an accident in which nobody had been injured, but they could have been, and as far as Murdoch was concerned the fault was on the part of Thomas Marshall. By implication, this carelessness was extended to James Ducat, who as PLK on the Flannan Isles Station was failing to run a tight ship and allowing sloppy practices under his command. Whilst Marshall may have sheepishly accepted that he had caused a near serious accident by failing to operate the crane properly, he could have only expected such a rebuke. The letter must have stung James Ducat however, particularly as the letter instructs him to read the contents of the letter verbatim to the other men under his command. In Ducat's repeating of the letter to them, the other keepers could not have failed to note the implied rebuke to their principal from headquarters. The seriousness of the tone of Murdoch's letter should be understood in the context of the accident at Sule Skerry in which someone had died. The official circular of 18 February 1898[8] from NLB Secretary James Murdoch, which was sent to all stations, stated:

Sir,
Owing to the recent lamentable accident at Sule Skerry, through the collapse of the crane at the landing place, by which one of the seamen of the 'Pole Star'[9] lost his life, I am directed by the Commissioners of Northern Lighthouses to inform you that they hold their Principal Keepers at all Stations and the Keeper in charge at Rock Stations, responsible for seeing that the crane or hoisting gear (if any) and all lifting tackle, and fittings, are kept in a sound and efficient state, and are in every respect reliable. The Lightkeepers will therefore examine them carefully on all occasions before

use, and maintain them and everything in connection with them in an efficient state by painting and oiling etc., when required. Should the Principal Keeper or Assistant in charge be of opinion that anything in connection with the crane or other machinery requires renewal or repair, intimation of the same must be made to the Secretary at once, unless the repair is such as can be safely and properly executed by the Lightkeepers.

Please acknowledge receipt, and place this Circular in your scrap book for reference by yourself and your successors.

Your Obedient Servant,
James Murdoch
Secretary[10]

Not even a year had passed since the incident with the crane and the associated correspondence and rebuke from headquarters at George Street. The Flannans had experienced one of the most severe storms since the men had taken up station there and it is possibly with this background in mind that James Ducat and Thomas Marshall must have mulled over their decision to try and get down to the west landing as soon as they could to see what state it was in and whether the box of ropes and other tackle were still secure. A second incident involving damage or loss to NLB property was not something that either Ducat or Marshall would have wished to see as it would be both of their names involved in a second incident within a year, with almost certain penalties for a second bout of supposed negligence. The penalties could be fines and or demotions. As the lowest ranked lightkeeper and with less than a year in service, Donald Macarthur may have been less concerned about whatever his more senior and more experienced colleagues proposed to do about the equipment on the west landing. Muirhead noted in his report of 8 January 1901:

When the accident occurred, Ducat was wearing sea boots
and a waterproof, and Marshall sea boots and oilskins, and
as Moore assures me that the men only wore those articles
when going down to the landings, they must have intended,
when they left the station, either to go down to the landing
or the proximity of it.[11]

Some accounts of the reason the men may have ventured to
the west landing in such atrocious weather and conditions
mention a fine of 5s that had been imposed on James Ducat
some eight months beforehand. This was for damage to unsecured tackle on the Flannan Isles; the NLB had felt that he had
been negligent and had fined him accordingly. The source for
this account is most likely the interview with James Ducat's
daughter who was 98 at the time of her interview in 1990
with *The Times* newspaper.[12] (*See* Chapter 9)

Ducat, Marshall and Macarthur are certainly not the only
lightkeepers to have been washed away by a large wave. An
NLB lightkeeper at Hyskeir was swept to his death from a
bridge and drowned by a freak large wave, while a second
lightkeeper survived.[13] The author, Tony Parker, in his commendable book[14] on the life of lightkeepers, includes an
interview with a PLK who relates the story of a supernumary
lightkeeper who took his fishing rod to go fishing from the
door of the tower lighthouse at sea and was never seen again,
presumably washed away by a freak wave.

Although it may seem simplistic, the fast approach of a giant
wave sweeping the three men to their deaths is what many
people have alighted on as the most obvious answer.

The existence of giant single waves was long considered
to be a part of sea lore, with the sizes of the waves considered to be in direct proportion to the size of the yarn being
spun. Whilst the existence of large waves which are out of the
ordinary has never necessarily been doubted, the problem has
always been one of gaining accurate scientific measurements.
There was no shortage of anecdotal evidence by the crews of

ships or lighthouse keepers and other shore-based observers of these waves.

There are many examples of what giant waves have done to ships and lighthouses. It was regularly noted by lightkeepers on Eilean Mor that spray from breaking waves in stormy weather would reach as high as the lantern, 328ft above sea level. There is an interesting parallel to the Eilean Mor Lighthouse, some 300 miles to the south-west on the stormy and windswept coast of County Mayo, Ireland. The location and situation of the Eagle Island Station was in many ways very similar to the Eilean Mor Lighthouse in that both were a similar height above the sea, built on rocky islands and faced the same Atlantic storms sweeping in from the west. On Eagle Island in the early 1830s not one but two light towers were built, known as Eagle Island East and Eagle Island West. Some indication of the size and strength of the North Atlantic storms could be gauged from the fact that during construction of the west tower, a massive wave had swept over it and carried all the building materials into the sea. At this point the west tower was only two courses high, but the base of the tower stood 196ft above sea level at high tide. The wave had therefore reached the best part of 200ft with still enough strength to carry these loose but heavy building materials clean away back into the sea. Both towers were constructed 132 yards apart with both lanterns at exactly the same level, 220ft above sea level although the heights of the towers differed at 64ft for the west tower and 87ft high for the east tower.

The lights became operational on 29 September 1835 and when both lights were directly in line of sight (either the lights at night or the towers themselves in daytime), they guided vessels past all dangers from Blacksod Bay to Broadhaven. Living quarters for the lightkeepers and their families were built by both towers and with the knowledge of what had happened at the west tower when the wave had swept away all the building materials, a massive sea wall was built around both towers and the living accommodation of both. Despite the presence of this

Postcard of the Flannan Isles Station dated 1912, published by the Lighthouse Literature Mission (LLM), Belfast. (Christopher Nicholson)

Thomas Marshall, Second ALK, was one of the three men who disappeared on 15 December 1900. (Steven Gibbons)

William Beggs, who eventually replaced James Ducat as PLK on the Flannan Isles and devised a hook to attach keepers to the cranes when working on them. (Ian Begg & Catherine Mackie Quirk)

Thomas Marshall is first on the left. The others, from left to right, are believed to be Donald Macarthur, James Ducat and NLB Superintendent Robert Muirhead. This picture was taken at the Flannans during Muirhead's visit with his wife, one week before the three keepers disappeared on 15 December 1900 (Steven Gibbons)

Some of the labourers who had worked on the construction of the light station and ancillary facilities on Eilean Mor. Many men were from Lewis but others came from further away in Scotland, including the Borders and Aberdeen. (Liz Turner & Morag McFadden)

The approach to Eilean Mor and the west landing. (Chris Downer)

Assistant Lightkeeper Ron Ireland on Eilean Mor in the late 1960s. (Ron Ireland)

The difficulty of landing from a boat on most parts of Eilean Mor are well illustrated in this photo. Landings can only be carried out safely in calm seas. (Chris Downer)

The east landing crane. (Ron Ireland)

West landing. The crane platform is 70ft above sea level. (Ron Ireland)

West landing. Some idea of the scale can be seen by looking at the lightkeeper just below the landing stage. He is pulling in a lobster pot. (Ron Ireland)

West landing. The steps and the tramway leading to the top of the cliff from the crane platform. (Ron Ireland)

West landing. A present-day view of the steps and disused tramway leading to what was the crane platform. This point is approximately 110ft above sea level and it was here that Robert Muirhead noted that the turf had been torn up by a giant wave. (Chris Downer)

West landing, 1980. A view of damage caused by waves which would have reached up over 100ft as this point is above the former crane platform. (Iain Angus)

The Eilean Mor Lighthouse shortly after construction was completed around 1900. (Liz Turner & Morag McFadden)

The view from the light tower taken in the late 1960s. (Ron Ireland)

The MV *Pole Star* relief vessel with the stone chapel in the foreground, late 1960s. (Ron Ireland)

The east landing with a sedate sea, late 1960s. (Ron Ireland)

The stone chapel believed to have been used by St Flann, and used by Fowlers in later years for shelter. (Chris Downer)

The shore station at Breasclete. It was taken over by the council and made into flats. David Alan Stevenson had originally wanted to place the shore station for the Flannans at Stromness. (Ian Cowe)

The spray from the top of the wave seen here at the west landing is approximately 90ft above sea level. (Liz Turner & Morag McFadden)

This picture of the west landing was reportedly taken prior to the tragedy, around 1900. (Liz Turner & Morag McFadden)

Another view of the west landing, around 1900. (Courtesy of Liz Turner & Morag McFadden)

Breasclete shore station *c.* 1900. The raising of the flag on the mast could signify a number of things, including a visit by the superintendent or a royal occasion. (Courtesy of Liz Turner & Morag McFadden)

high wall, which came almost up to the level of both lanterns, the force of the huge seas still created problems. The lights had only been operational for less than four months when, during the course of a storm on 17 January 1836, a rock thrown up by the waves shattered one of the panes of glass in the lightroom of the west tower and extinguished the light. The lightkeepers were able to get the light working again within an hour. During the same storm, the dwellings of the lightkeepers were also severely damaged, which must have been traumatising as the families lived on the island during this time.

Further problems were in store from the waves when severe gales on the 5 and 6 February 1850 caused damage to lanterns of both the east and west towers, causing the lights to be extinguished. The lights were out for several days, as it was not possible to send out anyone to effect repairs because of the gales, which did not subside until 11 February.

Eleven years after the damage to both lights, at noon on 11 March 1861, the east tower was hit by waves which smashed twenty-three panes of glass and swept some of the lamps down the tower's inner steps. The reflectors were hit by broken glass, damaging them beyond repair, and so much water had hit the lightroom that it had cascaded down the inside of the tower and pooled at the bottom of the tower itself. The door entrance opened inwards into the tower but the lightkeepers were unable to open it because of the weight of water behind. They had to drill holes in the door to allow the water to escape before they could open it and gain access to see the extent of the damage. It was not until the following night that the lightkeepers were able to get the light working again and even then only with a fewer number of lamps and reflectors. It was enough, however, for the light to be considered operational and to continue its function as a guide to vessels in the area. What is sobering about this particular event is that a wave or waves had travelled 133ft up the cliffs before travelling a further 87ft to the top of the tower and still contained enough force to create the damage it did, as well as leaving enough water at the base of the tower – the weight of which must have been at least a couple of tons – to jam the door entrance.

Bad enough as it was, this damage to the east tower was a portent of what was to come. On 29 December 1894 a severe storm struck the west coast. Eagle Island was hit hard, as were other stations on the west coast of Ireland and further north, including the north-west coast of Scotland. The lighthouse on the Flannan Isles had not been built at this stage, but if it had it would undoubtedly have been affected by the storm on 29 December 1894. This time the storm not only smashed panes of glass and put out the light on the east tower of Eagle Island, but it also severely damaged the protecting sea wall, as well as causing substantial damage to the lightkeepers' dwellings. The damage to the accommodation was so bad that the families were forced to seek shelter in the east tower itself for the duration of the storm. It was not until the following day that their compatriots over in the west tower realised their plight and were able to offer help. Once the storm had subsided, the families were taken ashore and housed at the shore station in Belmullet.

The severe damage to the lightkeepers' accommodation (plus damage caused to the tower itself by earlier storms) at the east tower forced a rethink by the Irish Lighthouse Commissioners about the future of the station. Mr Douglas, the Commissioners' Engineer, inspected both stations after the storm and wrote a report in which he recommended that the east station should be abandoned. Concurrently with his recommendation about abandoning the east station, he also stated that he believed the west station should be improved. In the meantime it was agreed that the fixed light apparatus which had been removed from the Tory Island Lighthouse should be installed in the west tower on Eagle Island and that both the west lighthouse and the temporarily repaired east lighthouse should be kept running for a short period with the lightkeepers being accommodated at the West Lighthouse Station. This was a temporary solution. On 1 November 1895 a new dioptric first order light came into operation in the west tower and use of the east tower was discontinued. The east tower was reduced by 20ft so that it did not create a shadow for the light from the west tower. The light in the west tower was group occulting (a description of the rhythmic light pattern given by the light), which showed white towards the open sea and red towards land. Accommodation for the lightkeepers and their families was built at Corclough on the Termoncarragh Road ,close to a point where the keepers could signal the station on the island by semaphore. The families were able to move into the new shore dwellings at the end of 1900.

Despite the improvements to the west station, another severe storm on 25 January 1935 again put the light out of action, although the lightkeepers were able to keep the fog signal going as some kind of a temporary solution for which they were commended.[15]

The shore dwellings were abandoned in 1955 and sold off in 1956 and from 1969 reliefs were carried out by helicopter, landing the lightkeepers at Blacksod. This replaced the long-established method of relief using a contractor's boat from Scotchport, 2 miles south of Eagle Island on the Mullet peninsula. Despite the improvements to the west station, further damage was caused in January 1987 and February 1988. On 31 March 1988, the lightkeepers were withdrawn and the lighthouse became fully automated.

Whilst it certainly would not be correct to say that massive seas had forced the Commissioners of the Irish lighthouses into abandoning a light station, due to the severity of the batterings it had taken, it had certainly forced a rethink on how the two Eagle Island towers could be better organised and run. The damage caused by the storm on 11 March 1861 to the east light tower showed that waves were capable of reaching up to a height of 220ft and causing damage; there was of course a serious risk to anybody hit by the water at that height. This is strongly worth taking into account when looking at what possibly happened to Ducat, Marshall and Macarthur. The highest point of Eilean Mor is only 8ft higher than the top of the east light tower on Eagle Island when it was hit in March 1861. The tops of the cliffs by the west landing on Eilean Mor are considerably lower than this, varying at points approximately between 110ft to 170ft.

In addition to the battering taken by lighthouses from giant waves, there is a long list of ships which have also suffered, and the size of the ships was no guarantee against their being sunk by monster waves. There are several well-known examples of sizeable ships being damaged or sunk. One of the most prominent cases occurred in 1978 to a German vessel, the MS *München*. The *München* was a LASH[16] vessel (the only one of her kind under the then West German flag) owned by the West German line Hapag Lloyd. She was a reasonably large vessel by any standard, 44,600 tons, and was launched on 12 May 1972 at the shipyards of Cockerill at Hoboken in Flanders, Belgium and delivered on 22 September 1972. On 7 December 1978 the *München* departed the port of Bremerhaven, with a crew of twenty-eight, to sail for Savannah, Georgia, carrying a cargo of steel products stored in eighty-three lighters on the vessel. She also carried a replacement nuclear reactor-vessel head for the American company Combustion Engineering, Inc. The trip to Savannah was a regular run for the *München* and the trip was to have been her sixty-second voyage. The weather ahead of the ship was not good, there was a severe storm which had started in November and had shown no signs of abating. However, the *München* had sailed through similar weather and sea conditions previously, plus the design of LASH vessels was such that they were considered to have exceptional floating capabilities. Despite the severe storm, the *München* made steady progress until just after midnight on the night of 12–13 December. The *München*'s radio officer, Jörg Ernst, made a short radio communication to a colleague named Heinz Löhmann on the German cruise ship *Caribe* which was a considerable distance away, 2,400 nautical miles. In the communication which he sent on a 'chat' frequency, Ernst stated that they were encountering bad weather and, more pertinently, he said that there had been damage to the *München*. Ernst also stated the last known position of the ship, which was some considerable distance into the Atlantic from the European mainland. The quality of the transmission was not good but as it was sent as a standard communication on a 'chat' frequency, the information was not passed back to Hapag Lloyd, the *München*'s owners, until four days later (17 December). Three hours after the communication from Ernst to Löhmann, partial SOS signals in Morse code were received by a Greek freighter *Marion*, which in turn relayed the SOS signals to a Soviet freighter *Marya Yermolova* and a West German tugboat *Titan*. The position of the *München* given by the signals was later believed to be approximately 100 miles (160km) away from her actual position. What added to the difficulty of getting a clear picture of what was happening was that only parts of the signals were actually being received. One part of the signal stated '50 degrees Starboard' which was taken to mean a 50-degree list to Starboard.

After the receipt of the SOS signals, at 4.43 a.m. a number of radio stations started to receive automatic emergency signals. At 5.30 p.m. on 13 December 1978 an international search and rescue operation commenced, controlled by the coastguard at Land's End in the UK. Three aircraft and six ships commenced a search for the *München*, but wind speeds with a strength of 11–12[17] on the Beaufort Scale hindered the effort.

A further signal was received at 9.06 a.m. on 13 December when a Belgian radio amateur in Brussels, named Michael Sinnot, received a voice transmission on the unusual frequency, 8238.4 kHz, which was usually used by the German ground station Norddeich Radio. The transmission was clear but interrupted by some noise, and contained parts of *München*'s name and call sign. Later, in court, Sinnot reported that the voice was calm and spoke in English but with a distinct German accent. Since Sinnot only had a receiver for this frequency, he relayed the message via telex to a radio station in Ostend. More signals were received later that day when ten weak Mayday calls were received by the US Naval Station at Rota in Spain at regular intervals, mentioning 'twenty-eight persons on board'. The messages may have been recorded and sent automatically. *München*'s call sign (DEAT), sent in Morse code, was received three times on the same frequency.

The weak Mayday calls were also received by a Dutch ocean-going tugboat *Smit Rotterdam*, which was returning from other mayday calls in the Gulf of Breton and the English Channel. The *Smit Rotterdam* immediately proceeded to the position given in the signals and acted as a coordination point for the ships and aircraft that were by that point involved in the search for the *München*. The weather was still bad with very heavy seas. The following day, 14 December, the wind speed had dropped to Force 9 and by this time there were seventeen ships and four aircraft involved in the search. Over the following days, 14–17 December, a number of ships located various items from the *München*. On 14 December signals were received from *München*'s emergency buoy and at 7 p.m. that day the British freighter *King George* picked up an empty life raft. Another Hapag Lloyd vessel, the *Erlangen*, found three of the eighty-three lighters that the *München* was carrying. In addition to the finds by the ships, an RAF Nimrod maritime reconnaissance aircraft located two orange objects in the sea, which were found to be buoys from the *München*.

Other ships in the search continued to find more items from the *München*. A life raft was found by a salvage tug *Titan* and another was found by the *MS Badenstein*. The weather had improved considerably by 17 December with the wind speed coming down to Force 3. On that afternoon the *Dusseldorf Express* found the *München*'s emergency buoy and a freighter named *Starlight* found two lifebelts and sighted three life vests. A fourth empty life raft was picked up by the *Sealand Consumer* and the *Evelyn* sighted another life vest. The search, which had been the largest undertaken to that date with thirteen aircraft and almost eighty ships, was then called off on the evening of 20 December 1978. The West German government and the *München*'s owners continued the search for a further two days along with support from US and British forces. Nothing further was found, however, and the search was completely called off.

Two months later, on 16 February 1979, a highly significant find was made by car transporter *Don Carlos*. The *Don Carlos* came across a lifeboat from the starboard side of the *München*, and this lifeboat was to play a central part in the investigation into what had happened to the ship.

What was deduced was that the pins in the forward block from which the starboard lifeboat hung had been bent back from fore to aft, when they should have been vertical. This implied that the lifeboat itself had been hit by a massive force which appeared to have run from fore to aft of the ship and torn the lifeboat away. The lifeboat was 66ft above the waterline. At this time the existence of such giant or rogue waves in deep water was considered to be almost statistically impossible. Nevertheless, what had hit the lifeboat could only have been such a wave, and the conclusion was drawn that the severe weather had somehow created an unusual event or phenomenon that had led to the sinking of the *München*.

As time passed and research continued into the formation and characteristics of giant waves, it was accepted that the *München* must have been hit by such a wave. Investigators drew the conclusions that as the ship made her way through the storm on the night of 12 December 1978, she came up against a giant wall of water which must have been between 80 to 100ft high. It would have been a terrifying sight. The ship would have first gone into the trough of the wave and not had time to rise out of the trough before the immense weight of the wave crashed down on to the ship. The force of the wave would have torn the starboard lifeboat away, smashed the bridge and broken windows and flooded the vessel. In the storm, this would have been the beginning of the end for the ship. With the loss of the bridge and steering, her engines would have been incapacitated and she would have drifted broadside into the waves. From the distress signals being sent out, the ship seems to have stayed afloat for some hours and it seems likely that she was then hit by another giant wave which would have either capsized or flooded her to such an extent that she sank within a very short period of time.[18]

Another well-known case worth looking at as one of the theories regarding its sinking involves the phenomenon of large waves known as the 'Three Sisters' (*see* p. 138).

The system of Great Lakes in North America is large enough to sustain its own regular fleets and passages of large freighters, known as Great Lakes Freighters. These freighters were used to mainly carry various types of iron ore around the various ports of the Great Lakes. One of these freighters, the SS *Edmund Fitzgerald*, was the largest of its kind when it was launched on 8 June 1958 and held the title of 'Queen of the Lakes' until the following year when an even larger vessel was launched, thereby taking the title. The *Edmund Fitzgerald* gained a reputation among boat watchers, for her captain was always piping various types of music through the ship's tannoy system as she made her way through the various locks around the Great Lakes. The *Edmund Fitzgerald* was known affectionately by her nicknames of *Fitz*, *Big Fitz* or *Mighty Fitz* for the various records the ship had broken.

Seamen are known for their superstition and the launching of the *Edmund Fitzgerald* was accompanied by some ill omens. It took three attempts to break the champagne bottle on her bow and it took shipyard workers a full thirty-six minutes to release the keel blocks for the actual launch to take place and immediately after the launch she collided with a pier. For an ore carrier, she was well fitted out with what was considered to be virtual luxury for the crew, including deep-pile carpets in their quarters and drapes over portholes. The ship also carried passengers as company guests. They were treated to candlelight dinners with the Captain and served by waiters in mess jackets. With some irony, in 1969 the *Edmund Fitzgerald* received a safety award which covered eight years of operations without a member of the crew having a single day off on account of work related injury. However, she ran aground that same year, and then the following year struck another vessel, the SS *Hochlelaga*. In 1970, 1973 and 1974, she hit the wall of a lock and in 1974 she lost her bow anchor in the Detroit River. Whilst none of these accidents were necessarily considered unusual, it could be argued that she had become an accident-prone vessel, despite the relatively minor nature of some of them.

On 9 February 1975, the *Edmund Fitzgerald*, with a crew of twenty-nine, left the port of Superior, Wisconsin, carrying a full cargo (26,116 long tons[19]) of ore pellets to the steel mill on Zug Island, close to Detroit. She was joined on the journey by another Great Lakes ore carrier, SS *Arthur M Anderson*, which had left the port of Two Harbors, Minnesota, for Gary, Indiana. The two ships then proceeded together and the following day, they ran into a storm with hurricane-force winds. Accompanying the extremely high winds were waves up to 35ft high. Shortly after 7.10 p.m. the *Edmund Fitzgerald* suddenly sank, 17 miles from the entrance to Whitefish Bay, near to the cities of Sault Ste Marie, Michigan and Sault Ste Marie, Ontario. She sank in water which was 530ft deep and all hands on board perished. No bodies were ever recovered.

A number of theories were put forward as to what caused this large ship to sink. One of the theories which is considered to be the most plausible is a combination of giant waves and the weather. At the time of the sinking the *Edmund Fitzgerald* had entered an area on Lake Superior which had very high winds (the *Arthur M Anderson* had reported winds up to 57mph) with some waves reaching up to a height of 47ft. A computer simulation was run in 2005 which showed gusts of wind up to 86mph in the area where the *Edmund Fitzgerald* sank.

One possibility put forward is that a rogue wave phenomenon known as the 'Three Sisters' occurred in the area at the time the ship sank. The 'Three Sisters' phenomenon is three rogue waves close together and on average one third higher than all the waves surrounding them. It is surmised that these hit the ship one after another. The first one probably hit the ship and swamped it and before the water had time to drain away, she was hit in rapid succession by two more of these huge waves which caused her to sink immediately. The deck would have become overloaded with literally many tons of water, which the ship could not sustain.

To give some credence to the 'Three Sisters' wave possibility, the Captain of the *Arthur M. Anderson* had reported that his ship had been hit by two 30–35ft (10m) waves which had buried the aft cabins and damaged a lifeboat. The second of the waves had gone over the bridge deck and the captain stated that these waves were possibly followed by a third large wave, had continued in the direction of the *Edmund Fitzgerald*. In the few hours before she sank, Captain McSorley of the *Edmund Fitzgerald* had been in radio communication with the US Coast Guard and the *Arthur M. Anderson*. He had reported at 3.30 p.m. that day that his ship was taking on water and that she was listing as well as having lost two vent covers and a fence railing. More seriously the ship had lost the use of both radars. Very early that same morning, the weather service had upgraded the weather status from gales to a storm warning.

That afternoon, the weather worsened and the waves increased in height. It was in this considerably weakened state, with a severe list, that the ship was hit by the 'Three Sisters'. The last communication with Captain McSorley was at 7.10 p.m. when the captain of the *Arthur M. Anderson* contacted him to ask how he was doing. McSorley's response was 'We are holding our own'. The ship sank almost immediately after this exchange. Ten minutes later the captain of the *Arthur M. Anderson* could not raise her on the radio or see her on the radar.

The loss of the *Edmund Fitzgerald* was highly significant for a number of reasons, not least being the suddenness of her loss, and thus has attracted a great deal of interest. She was the largest vessel to have sunk in the Great Lakes and the findings from her loss led to a number of changes in shipping regulations on the lakes, including more frequent inspections of vessels, depth finders, increased freeboard, positioning systems and mandatory survival suits.[20]

It may come as a surprise, considering how long man has encountered giant waves, but the causes of rogue waves are still the subject of active research. It is important to separate giant or rogue waves from tidal waves, which are a completely different phenomenon. It is still too early to say that there are any firm conclusions as to what the common causes of these rogue waves are or whether the waves vary from one place to another. Rogue waves appear in bad weather conditions when the average wave height is high and several large waves come together to create a monster. They can also happen in sea conditions with smaller average-sized waves, but because the average height is small, the bigger wave tends to get overlooked because it does not stand out. There appear to be four main reasons for the formation of the giant waves: when the wind pushes against a strong current (one notable location for this occurrence is off the coast of South Africa); when a shallow sea bottom focuses waves to one spot (for example off the coast of Norway); purely by chance; and when waves become unstable and start to self-focus. Scientific study appears to show that the giant waves encountered in areas of deep ocean like the Pacific and North Atlantic are due to unstable waves self-focusing in conditions of bad weather. Their research has shown that there appears to be a population of unstable waves in the ocean which can grow into monster waves.

Whilst monster waves can appear anywhere, there are certain areas where they can be predicted, including off the east coast of South Africa where the South African weather service gives freak wave warnings. There, a strong wind blows in the opposite direction to the strong Agulhas current, which is one of the conditions for creating giant waves. The bottom of the sea just off the coast of Norway is another place where giant waves can occur, as the sea bottom appears to focus waves together to create extremely large ones. When this happens, ships are alerted to alter their routes in order to avoid the affected area.[21] The vastness of the Pacific is also notorious for massive waves, which can be caused by typhoons. One of the best-known cases involved the British bulk carrier *Derbyshire* which sank in a typhoon south of Japan on 9 September 1980. The *Derbyshire* was sailing from Sept-Îles in Canada to Kawasaki, Japan, carrying a cargo of 157,446 tonnes of iron ore. When 230 miles from Okinawa, she hove to in Typhoon *Orchid*. The giant ore carrier was believed to have sunk in a matter of minutes without any distress call being sent. All forty-two crew plus two women married to crew members were lost. She was, and still remains, the largest British ship ever to have been lost at sea.[22]

Although the investigation concluded that the *Derbyshire* sank because of structural failure, it was giant seas which had battered the front part of the ship combined with open ventilator panels in the bow section of the ship which led directly to the ship filling up with water and eventually a catastrophic failure of the hull. Douglas Faulkner, Professor of Marine Architecture and Ocean Engineering at Glasgow University, concluded that a freak wave or waves had also played a part in the destruction of the ship.[23]

What has assisted greatly in wave research in more recent times is the use of satellite technology and computer modelling. Research has been carried out by many institutions and universities including research at Umea University in Sweden. One of the main intentions of the research is to find out not just what causes these giant waves, but to also see if they can be predicted by location and time in order to make it safer for ships. It was traditionally thought that these giant or rogue waves occurred once every ten thousand years, but as time went on, the sightings became more frequent.

One event was to change perceptions completely, as it

was possible to scientifically measure the event known as the 'Draupner Wave'. On New Year's Day, 1 January 1995 the Draupner oil rig in the North Sea was hit by a 98ft, giant wave. Minor damage was recorded on the platform and the rogue wave was measured to a good degree of accuracy. The 'Draupner Wave', despite its immense size of 98ft, was certainly not the largest wave ever seen, but it was the first wave which was actually scientifically measured. It may seem surprising, but, despite the history of seafaring spanning a number of centuries and countless accounts of giant waves, up until the 'Draupner Wave', not one had been scientifically measured with correct accuracy. Satellite technology has helped considerably in studying giant waves and in 2004 scientists using three weeks of radar data from the European Satellite Agency found ten rogue waves of 82ft or more. In February 2000 a British oceanography vessel in the Rockall Trough west of the Flannan Isles recorded waves with standard heights of 61ft and individual waves up to 95ft.

Without going into great detail, the scientific study of the waves is broken into six areas: diffractive focusing, focusing by currents, nonlinear effects (modulationary instability), normal part of the wave programme, wind waves, and thermal expansion.

Broadly speaking, rogue waves can be divided into three main groups: walls of water, 'Three Sisters'; and single giant storm waves. It should be mentioned that freak waves are different to tsunamis. Tsunamis are caused by a mass displacement such as a movement of the ocean floor caused by an earthquake. They move at high speeds and only become dangerous as they approach the shoreline when the depth of the water becomes shallower. Tsunamis tend to get more media coverage as they affect large areas of inhabited coastlines on a regular basis, causing immense damage and loss of life which is comparatively easy to record and verify. By contrast, giant waves are not so easy to record as they tend to occur far out to sea and in remote areas usually far from regular sealanes, although, as has been mentioned, in the case of the *München* and the *Edmund Fitzgerald,* they also occur regularly on shipping routes.

There is no doubt that a number of lightkeepers who were stationed on Eilean Mor through the years would have long pondered the fate of their fellow lightkeepers on 15 December 1900. One lightkeeper in particular became totally preoccupied with the missing lightkeepers to the extent that it became almost an obsession.

Walter Robert Aldebert was born on 27 September 1908, almost eight years after the tragedy. He became a seaman but applied to join the NLB and was accepted as a supernumerary lightkeeper on 15 May 1929. He was first posted to Inchkeith for his training where he spent four months before moving onto Macarthur's Head on 23 September 1929. Shortly after his move there, on 3 October 1929, he was promoted to ALK. He spent three years and five months at Macarthur's Head and over the next almost twenty years he was posted to, in turn: Ardnamurchan, Tarbertness, Sule Skerry, Rhinns of Islay and Stour Head. From his arrival at Stour Head, he was to spend five years and five months there and during that time he was promoted to PLK on 1 October 1949. From Stour Head he moved on to the Flannan Isles, arriving there on 4 June 1953, and it was during his time on Eilean Mor that he spent much time looking down on the west landing and out to sea, particularly during stormy weather. When the waves were particularly large, he would place himself in precarious positions to take photographs. In total he took over thirty rolls of film. By the time he left the Flannan Isles, after spending four years and three months there, Aldebert had given a considerable amount of thought to what had happened to Ducat, Marshall and Macarthur. He came up with a completely different theory to the standard one, long accepted, that all three men had gone down to the west landing and had been swept away by a single giant wave. His view was that for a three-man station, one always had to remain within the station (certainly not always adhered to) and that only Ducat and Marshall had gone down to the west landing on 15 December 1900 to check the box of ropes and tackle were still secure. Aldebert did not believe the weather was storm force with corresponding wave sizes on that day, but rather that there would have been a heavy swell with fairly large waves hitting the west landing. He believed that Ducat and Marshall were checking the west landing and one of them had lost his footing and fallen into the sea. Seeing his colleague in the swell, the other probably felt it would be better to have two of them trying to get the third out of the water. So either Ducat or Marshall (whichever of the two had not lost his footing and fallen into the water) probably shouted to whoever was in the sea that he was going to get Macarthur to come and help him and ran back up the steps of the west landing to the station and shouted to Macarthur to come and help him. Aldebert felt that this would explain why Macarthur would have gone out in his shirtsleeves, as time would have been of the essence. With the third man in the sea, the two would have gone down as close as possible to try and get him out. Whilst they were doing this, a large wave arrived and, before they had time to scramble clear, the other two men were swept into the sea and all three drowned.

Aldebert put his theory into a report and, along with the thirty-plus rolls of film he had taken of the sea and waves on the Flannans, he lodged them with the NLB headquarters at 84 George Street. He moved onto St Abbs Head from the Flannan Isles in 1957 and after spending eight years (the longest he spent at any station), his final posting was Cromarty where he arrived on 6 September 1965 and spent two years and eleven months, finally retiring on 30 September 1968. Walter Aldebert has now passed away but his theory is probably a far better explanation of what actually happened to Ducat, Marshall and Macarthur, and it was a theory developed over a number of years on the actual location itself. Unfortunately there is no trace of Aldebert's rolls of film and report, either at 84 George Street or the National Archives of Scotland, who have clearly stated that they do not have them. Should the report and rolls of film ever surface, it would be of great interest to researchers.

There is also an interesting incident which helps to back-up the possibility of the wave or waves sweeping Ducat, Marshall and Macarthur to their deaths from the west landing on Eilean Mor. An NLB lightkeeper, Jack Ross, was actually stationed on the Flannan Isles when he encountered something very similar. He recounted[24] a day when he was walking down by the west landing on Eilean Mor when a giant wave appeared from 'nowhere', as he later put it, and hit the three of them (he and his two fellow keepers). They were fortunate that they had seen the approach of the wave, but despite this they did not have enough time to gain height and get out of its way, so they grabbed whatever supports they could to gain some kind of a purchase. Ross stated that the wave hit them like the proverbial brick wall and had they not been prepared for its approach by grabbing hold of something, all three of them would have been swept into the sea and probably drowned.

The experience of Ross and his companions confirms what Muirhead concluded in his written report shortly afterwards. It was Jack Ross's firm belief until his dying day that had the three of them not managed to grab hold of various supports, there would have been another Flannan Islands Lighthouse mystery. The disappearance and loss of another three lightkeepers on Eilean Mor seventy years after the first disappearance certainly would have made for some interesting reading in the news.

Finally, there is the possibility of a local wave phenomenon. A local man named Niall Beag had worked on the Eilean Mor Lighthouse during its construction phase and features in a photograph taken on the island when the construction was being carried out. He referred to a phenomenon known as the *Muir Cul*, which was a giant wave created by a succession of days with an east to west momentum of the sea, followed by a change in wind to the opposite direction (i.e. west to east, which are the prevailing winds in this area). The fairly abrupt change in its early stages has the wind blowing one way with the sea going in the opposite direction, leading to the state known as a *Muir Cul* (sea from the back) when waves of above average size are created but are totally unexpected. A further elaboration of the *Muir Cul* comes from Iain Angus, who has worked all his life on the sea in this area. He describes it as when the sea comes from behind you when on a point or rock. This can be when fishing from the rock and watching the sea in front of you, but a large swell approaching unseen from behind comes right over the rock or point and will wash you into the sea. He stated that this did not happen at the Flannans as no sea of that magnitude from the north-east could come over the island without being felt elsewhere in the Hebrides. He states that there is one place on the Flannans, however, where the sea appears to come over from the north towards the west landing on a small scale in violent storms, but it is in fact spray blown from a high geo and a small river that has stone boulders bordering it — this is not where the men would have been working.

Notes

1. The terms giant, rogue, freak and monster are all interchangeable in reference to very large waves.
2. Report by Superintendent Robert Muirhead, 8 January 1901, Scottish National Archives file no. NL/3/1/1.
3. Meteorological Office Archives Exeter, see Appendix III.
4. Account of visit by a minister to Flannan Isles Lighthouse, April 1900, in *Scotsman*, 29 December 1900.
5. Ibid.
6. Letter from NLB Secretary James Murdoch to PLK James Ducat, 11 April 1900, Scottish National Archives file no. NL/3/1/1.
7. Ibid.
8. Official circular from NLB Secretary James Murdoch to all stations, 18 February 1898, Scottish National Archives file no. NL/3/1/1.
9. *Pole Star* was the then lighthouse relief vessel for the NLB.
10. Official circular from NLB Secretary James Murdoch to all stations, 18 February 1898, Scottish National Archives file no. NL/3/1/1.
11. Report by Superintendent Robert Muirhead, 8 January 1901, Scottish

National Archives file no. NL/3/1/1.
12 Interview ,'Boxing Day on Flannan Rock', with Anna Ducat by Joan Simpson, *The Times*, 26 December 1990.
13 *Stargazing* by Peter Hill, Canongate Books, 2003, p. 250.
14 *Lighthouse* by Tony Parker, Eland Publishing, 1986, pp. 45–8.
15 See www.cil.ie.
16 LASH, an acronym for Lighter Aboard Ship, i.e. a vessel designed to carry barges.
17 11 on the Beaufort Scale denotes exceptionally high waves. Very large patches of foam, driven before the wind, cover much of the sea surface. Very large amounts of airborne spray severely reduce visibility, with waves up to 52ft.
18 The loss of the *München* was featured in an edition of the BBC documentary series *Horizon* entitled 'Freak Wave', which was first shown on 14 November 2002. In 2003, the Science Channel made a documentary about killer waves that included the disappearance of the *München* and concluded that a rogue wave was the most likely cause of her loss.
19 A long ton is the name for the unit called the ton in the imperial system of measurement that was used in the UK before metrification. One long ton is equal to 2,240lb (1,016 kg). It is still used in the USA for measuring the displacement of ships.
20 See en.wikipedia.org/wiki/SS_Edmund_Fitzgerald.
21 See www.bbc.co.uk/science/horizon/2002/freakwaveqa.shtml.
22 See en.wikipedia.org/wiki/MV_Derbyshire.
23 Ibid.
24 Story recounted to NLB Lightkeeper Alistair Henderson by Jack Ross himself, and recounted to the author.

MURDER

Following on from the most popular theory that Ducat, Marshall and Macarthur fell victim to a giant wave, the next contender for a theory of what happened to the three men is the possibility of foul play of some kind.

While the idea that one lightkeeper had gone berserk and killed his co-workers may be dismissed as preposterous by some, it is not as outlandish a theory as one might think, as there are enough examples of difficulties with lightkeepers in their lonely places of work where problems have arisen and ended very badly. There is also an example on the Eilean Mor lighthouse itself which shows that the potential for violence was actually a very real possibility. Donald John Macleod (Domhnall Iain a' Chidhe as he was known locally - 'Donald John of the Quay' literally,[1] but spoken of as Donald John Quayhouse in spoken English), worked as the harbour master at Breasclete from the 1930s onwards. He was never officially appointed as harbour master; instead he appeared to just fall into the role, as the family lived adjacent to the pier. However, he fulfilled the role substantially and was the contact for many agencies, including customs and excise, the coastguard, and trawler and shipping companies. For the last twenty years or more of his life, he ran his own business providing services to trawlers from all over Europe who worked off the west coast of Lewis. He became well known through the years. A former colleague of his son was on a visit to the Faroe Islands in the mid-1980s and met the prime minister of the islands at a function. On telling the prime minister that he came originally from Lewis, the prime minister asked 'Do you know my old friend Donald Macleod at the Quay House in Breasclete?'

Donald John Macleod's father, also called Donald, had not only been Breasclete Harbour Master before him but had also been involved in the construction of the lighthouse on Eilean Mor from 1896 to 1899.

Donald John (the son) was actually working on the Eilean Mor Lighthouse on the day the Second World War broke out in September 1939. He is sometimes referred to as the 'part-time' harbour master for Breasclete because he also served as an OLK on the Flannan Isles Lighthouse, therefore almost combining the two jobs with each being considered part-time, although he spent far more time as Breasclete Harbour Master than as an OLK on the Flannans. The point of an OLK was to be available to fill in on the Flannans in case one of the lightkeepers there became sick or indisposed in some way.

On one occasion Donald John MacLeod described[2] how, while he was working on Eilean Mor, one of the lightkeepers had a mental breakdown and the other lightkeeper was severely incapacitated with flu. He tried to keep everything running on his own until the arrival of the relief on the *Pole Star* which was four days away, coming from Stromness via Breasclete. The mentally unstable lightkeeper had threatened violence to both MacLeod and the other lightkeeper incapacitated by flu, which resulted in them having to overpower the out-of-control lightkeeper and tie him up. MacLeod's view was that this could have been a possibility in the case of the disappearance of the missing lightkeepers, as he had himself feared the behaviour of the mentally disturbed lightkeeper.[3]

Whilst foul play may seem unlikely at first sight, one must look at the nature of lighthouse work to consider the context in which foul play could arise.

When a layman thinks of the life of a lighthouse man, usually one of the first things that comes to mind is the sense of isolation and deprivation, the sense of an individual physically alone and far away from human contact. It has to be said that this view is not necessarily correct but it does lean in the right direction that lighthouse keepers, by the very nature of the job, are isolated for the most part due to their place of work. While some lights were fairly close to towns or large places of settlement (such as the Isle of Man), many were on rocks several miles offshore or on small islands (such as Eilean Mor on the Flannan Isles). It may seem odd that some lightkeepers found that some of the mainland stations actually felt more isolated than the rock stations, but this was the case.

There is another occupation which has close parallels with lightekeeping in terms of the monotony of work, the isolation of being cooped up for lengthy periods with a couple of colleagues, and the physical distance from the nearest habitation. It may surprise some, but the psychological aspects of space travel since its earliest days have come to closely resemble the conditions experienced by working lighthousemen. Numerous studies have described the boredom and psychological pressures of space travel. Whilst space flights are generally now longer than the original expeditions made by the likes of astronaut Yury Gagarin and the Apollo missions, it was found that in missions of more than one and a half month's orbit, there were three problems encountered.[3] Two of them (the effect of microgravity on physiology and radiation) are unrelated, but the third problem, the psychological effect of space travel, is closely connected to similar issues affecting the life of lighthouse keepers.

The leading medical cause of the termination of some long-duration missions has been due to what has been termed 'psychosocial issues'. Doctor Jay C. Buckey Jr,[4] a former astronaut and medic, has studied this problem in depth and concluded that the issue of close confinement and proximity to other crew members on a mission can lead to major psychological problems, with depression foremost among them. For their 'Bioinfomatics Road Map', which NASA use to try to identify and assess the risks to the crews of exposure to space travel, the problem of psychosocial issues is given as 'Priority One' for potential missions to Mars and working on an international space station. In other words, the psychological problems of a small number of people cooped up with each other in a relatively confined space for long periods of time without a break is given the highest priority in planning space missions of any duration. By comparison, little or no thought was given to similar psychological issues arising from lighthouse keepers spending lengthy periods of time similar to those experienced by astronauts in space travel. Three lightkeepers on a tower lighthouse in the middle of the sea were probably the closest scenario to astronauts' conditions, with regards to their proximity to each other and very limited scope for movement due to a restricted living area. The failure of a tender, for instance, to bring a relief to a lighthouse, therefore adding sometimes up to another month to the length of time the lightkeeper had to wait for his leave, brought added psychological stress to a lightkeeper who had already served a full rotation on the station. It may appear surprising that not a great deal of thought was given to this aspect of life on a lighthouse, but, certainly in the earlier days, more weight would be given to the more stoic type of personality who could shoulder responsibility and basically get on with what would be considered to be a hard life without grumbling about it. Had lighthouses continued to be manned up to the present day (2014), there is no doubt that psychometric testing of some form would have been introduced to weed out potentially unsuitable applicants from a psychological point of view. By the late 1960s many could see the writing on the wall with regard to the benefits of automation, although it was to be thirty more years before the last manned lighthouse was fully automated. Nevertheless, the first NLB lighthouse to be automated was Chicken Rock on the Isle of Man in 1971. Even at this point, new lighthouse keepers were still being taken on and their interviews and screening process amounted to little more than questions about whether they could cook plus one or two general questions about themselves. One newly appointed lightkeeper spoke of being back out on the street in front of the headquarters on George Street amazed at how short the interview had actually been.

From the foregoing, it can be seen that there is therefore plenty of potential for the build-up of tension. Most of the tension, depression and any other psychological issues would dissipate themselves in the form of arguments, pranks and other ways of letting off steam through hobbies and work. However, the potential was there for less stable personalities, who were unable to focus their thoughts and energies in other directions, to turn to violence when tensions boiled over. It has to be said that this would rarely happen, but the earlier NLB registers of lighthouse keepers show a number of dismissals for assault including one on a PLK's wife.

One of the earliest accounts of a supposed murder took place on Scotland's first lighthouse on the Isle of May when the first lightkeeper there drowned and Effie Lang of Anstruther was burned as a witch for the 'crime'.[5]

That one lightkeeper might turn on a fellow keeper in a murderous rage is certainly within the bounds of possibility and there are examples around the world including one within the NLB's own domain.

On 18 August 1960 David Collin,[6] who was an architecture student at the Edinburgh College of Art, left the slipway of the Kirkcudbright Sailing Club in a 13ft dinghy, with his father, to visit Little Ross Island. They reached the island, with its lighthouse, just before lunchtime and left their dinghy at the east quay. After they arrived they walked over to the west quay, which had an old shelter that was used as a garage for the island's motor van. The two of them had their lunch there and once finished they decided that, as a matter of courtesy, they should pay a visit to the Ross Island Lighthouse and at least let the lightkeepers know they were on the island. The lighthouse station on Little Ross had two keepers cottages and David Collin and his father knocked on the doors of both of them but received no response. The only sign of life was a friendly dog, which followed them around, and Collin would mention years later that something did not seem to be right about the scene when they arrived on it. Initially, he and his father were worried that they were disturbing the lightkeepers off-duty, as there appeared to be no sign of life at the place. The only sound they heard was the sound of a ringing telephone. He then heard another noise coming from a box. He lifted the box to find a rabbit, suffering from the heat of being trapped in the box, and sensing its freedom it hopped away. It must have seemed like an ill omen, and as time wore on the two men became puzzled by the total lack of any activity or signs of life. Collin's father decided to take the plunge and go into one of the cottages. In his account of the incident, Collin mentioned his embarrassment at his father's well-intentioned foray onto the private property of the lightkeepers. The first cottage that the senior Mr Collin went into was the PLK's cottage. There seemed to be nothing untoward inside, so he came out and went into the other cottage, which belonged to the ALK. Mr Collin senior immediately came out of the ALK's cottage and shouted to his son to go and get help as he had found a man in bed who was either very ill or possibly dead.

David Collin ran back to the east quay where they had left their boat and shouted to people he knew who were in a boat out on the water. David Collin and one of the two from the boat returned to the ALK's cottage and went in. Mr Collin senior guided the two men to a small bedroom on the west side of the cottage where a man lay in a bed with his head wrapped in a towel and his feet and legs protruding. There was blood near the man's head and what David Collin found odd was that there were lengths of rope lying on the bed. The person who had arrived with Collin left to go back to his elderly father on the west quay and Mr Collin senior rang both the police and a doctor. He was told to stay put and to wait with his son until help arrived and his suggestion to take the injured man to Ross Bay, where he could be collected, was declined. The authorities contacted George Poland who commanded the NLB's launch to take them out to Little Ross Island.

David Collin and his father settled down for what turned out to be a considerable wait. In his account of that afternoon Collin mentions some unsettling details. On their arrival at the island, they had noticed an abandoned dinghy near the mouth of Ross Bay, which they resolved to look at later on. Rather than stay right by the lifeless body, the two wandered around the lighthouse station in a state of great unease. Another look inside the PLK's cottage again showed nothing unusual. There was a budgie in its cage and nothing appeared out of place. However, one thing in particular made them wary. When they went into the workshop at the base of the tower they found the sawn off barrel of a rifle in a vice. They also found that the last entry in the station log book had been at 3 a.m. and wondered why there had been no entry since then. Their thoughts turned to the abandoned dinghy at Ross Bay and they began to wonder if it belonged to the other keeper, who they surmised may have gone for help. The two men then went up to the top of the tower to await the arrival of the police and doctor. Eventually they saw the approach of the NLB launch with the expected help. They went down to the east quay to meet the launch. On board were two policemen plus a doctor and, bizarrely, a representative of the NLB who had come to officially inform the two lightkeepers on the Little Ross Island lighthouse that the station was going to be automated and would no longer be manned. The whole party then made its way up to the cottage and the body, and David Collin and his father gave their account of the afternoon.

An examination of the man in the bed by the doctor confirmed that he had died and the NLB official who had come to deliver the news regarding automation of the lighthouse, ran outside the cottage and was sick. It was also confirmed that the dead man was twenty-four-year-old relief lightkeeper Hugh Clark of Dalry. After answering questions put by the police, both David Collin and his father were allowed to leave. It was dark by the time they left the island, so they were towed back to Kirkcudbright harbour by the two people who had assisted them earlier in the day. When they arrived at the quay in Kirkcudbright, news photographers were already waiting for them and the men were subjected to a barrage of flashlights – news had obviously spread rapidly and great interest had been aroused, as there was obviously foul play of some kind involved. Within a short period of time, the missing ALK, named Robert Dickson, was found and arrested in Yorkshire.

Dickson went on trial for murder and theft at the High Court in Dumfries on 27 November 1960. David Collin and his father were called as witnesses during the trial. Whilst the evidence against Dickson was overwhelming, his defence was based on his actions being due to his being a psychopath and verging on insanity. The point was strongly made that he had severe adverse and abnormal reactions to stress. David Collin mentions in his account that the line of defence was very well put and that it was apparent to all the witnesses in court that it was an apt description of Dickson's behaviour. Nevertheless the jury found Dickson guilty of the charges and he was sentenced to death (this was some time prior to the abolition of capital punishment) by the presiding Judge, Lord Cameron. Collin notes in his account that as the death sentence was being made by Lord Cameron, in a scene which could have been taken from a Victorian melodrama, the courtroom grew darker and there was thunder and lightning outside. It was a fitting end to a strange case. However it was not quite the end; five days before he was due to be hanged on 21 December 1960, Dickson was reprieved. Two years later, in prison, Dickson committed suicide by taking an overdose of drugs. As an endnote to the account, Collin echoed sentiments that would be felt by many that, although it was a sad case which involved murder and suicide, looking back many years later after automation, equally regrettable was the loss of the traditions and way of life of the NLB's lightkeepers and their vigilance on behalf of seamen.[7]

Another case[8] while not concerning murder, is worth looking at as an example of madness or insanity overcoming a lightkeeper and the effect it had on him. Twenty-one miles off St David's Head in South Wales lay two small clusters of rock which had been a constant hazard to shipping until a lighthouse was built on one of the clusters. Placing a lighthouse there had been the inspiration of John Phillips, who invited designs for the construction. The design he chose for the lighthouse had been presented by Henry Whiteside, a music instrument maker from Liverpool. The two clusters of rocks, which stood at most 11.5ft above sea level, were known as the Smalls and this was the name given to the lighthouse. It was an isolated location and came under the jurisdiction of Trinity House through an Act of Parliament in 1778, although they leased it to Phillips for a period of ninety-nine years from 3 June 1778. The original lighthouse, built in 1775–76, was constructed primarily of wood and cast iron, and after severe storms in December 1777 Phillips had been forced to release the lightkeepers, as he could not afford to repair the lighthouse. The inability of Phillips to provide the necessary finance for repairs and running costs had forced the intervention of Trinity House.

It was in the Smalls Lighthouse just before 1801 that one of the two lightkeepers working there died, it is believed, of natural causes. The other lightkeeper was at a loss about what to do initially. He felt that if he did the most sensible thing, which was to commit the body of his deceased co-worker to the deep, he would have to explain what had happened. There was a strong possibility that he might not be believed in which case he would therefore run the risk of being accused of murder with no real way of proving his innocence.

It was well known that the two men, Tom Howells and Tom Griffiths, did not get on and intensely disliked each other. When on duty the two men argued constantly, sometimes quite ferociously. The unfortunate location of the Smalls Lighthouse and the relatively small size of it meant that neither man could get much of a break from the other and spent most of their time in close proximity. Even the usual pastimes when relaxing in a lighthouse, such as playing cards, would require one of the men to interact with the other in a sociable manner, and carrying out lighthouse work required both to cooperate whether they liked it or not. Fishing and reading were about the only two pursuits where each could do something without involving the other. Both would normally expect their relief to arrive after one month on duty. However with appalling winter weather and storms, the two were stuck on the lighthouse (and with each other) for four months. Although the two of them argued constantly and vociferously, no physical contact was involved, so there was no actual violence. One night, however, matters came to a head when in the middle of yet another furious row, Griffiths became so enraged he collapsed and fell to the floor, gashed his head on a metal lantern and died. Howells was therefore left with his dead colleague on the floor with no way of alerting the mainland directly of what had happened.

Howells's somewhat ingenious solution to the problem was to construct a makeshift coffin out of the wooden cupboards in the lighthouse. He then dragged the makeshift coffin up the circular steps of the lighthouse to lash the box itself with the dead body inside it, to the outside of the light tower, onto the lantern rails along with a distress flag. By doing this, the body was out of the confines of the interior once it started to decompose but it was at least proof, as far as Howells was concerned, that he had not murdered his colleague Griffiths. By taking the body outside, Howells had also hoped that the cold weather would also slow the decomposition of the body. A number of ships passed the lighthouse and saw the wooden box lashed to the lantern's rails (but not the supposed distress flag) which, it is reported, some observers thought odd but none of them did anything regarding investigating or reporting it. As time passed, Howells, left alone in the tower with the body lashed to the outside, slowly lost his mind and by the time the relief boat came for him, accounts have said that he was quite unhinged. Although there may be some journalistic licence involved, a contemporary report states that relief boats were unable to reach the lighthouse owing to the bad weather but the men on board could see that the waves had smashed the wooden box to pieces, and the decomposing body of Griffiths was hanging onto the lantern rail with an arm hooked over it. From a distance the men in the relief boat felt as if the decayed corpse of Griffiths was trying to wave them onto the rocks.

In the brief Trinity House account[9] of this incident, it is mentioned that three keepers were thereafter appointed to this lighthouse. It is taken as a generalisation that three keepers were always appointed to lighthouses across the British Isles from that point onwards as a result, but this was not always the case.

The Smalls Lighthouse itself was rebuilt over a period of five years, with completion in 1861. It was basically a completely new lighthouse built under the supervision of Trinity House engineer James Douglass, basing the design of the Smalls Lighthouse on Eddystone Tower.

Another incident[10] across the North Atlantic took place in early March 1880. Whilst this conflict came to a head in a fairly formal and ritualised manner – a duel – the outcome was still the same in that a lighthouse keeper died and the events leading up to his death had been caused by friction between the dead keeper and a colleague at the lighthouse. St Simons Island Lighthouse is on the southern tip of St Simons Island, Georgia, in the USA. It stands 208ft tall and was first lit in 1872 and automated as early as 1954. The original lighthouse, which was built in 1810, initially came under the control of Confederate troops during the American Civil War, who enforced a naval blockade of that section of coast. In 1862 Union troops invaded and forced the Confederates out of the area. Before they withdrew, the Confederate troops destroyed the lighthouse in order to stop it being of any use to the Unionists and their shipping. A new lighthouse was then built slightly to the west of the one which had been destroyed and it became operational in 1872. Two years after the new lighthouse became operational a new head keeper named Frederick Osborne arrived on the station. The descriptions of Osborne conjure up an image of a man who was a nit-picking and fastidious martinet for whom nothing was ever right. Osborne may have blended into an organisation like the army where orders had to be obeyed and obedience was expected, but such a character in the confines of a lighthouse, with minimal oversight and in charge of only one or two subordinates at most, was a recipe for disaster. There are two accounts of how the final confrontation came about in early March 1880. The first is that the nit-picking Osborne had made an inappropriate remark to the wife of assistant keeper John Stephens. Another version had the roles reversed with assistant keeper John Stephens making unwanted advances towards Osborne's wife. Whatever happened would appear to have involved the wives of one or both men and required that honour be satisfied. A duel between the two men was arranged and both men eventually faced each other 98ft apart. Osborne had a pistol and Stephens had a shotgun loaded with buckshot. The two men exchanged shots and Osborne was fatally wounded as a result. Criminal charges were brought against Stephens for killing Osborne, but he was acquitted. The matter did not end there however as the ghost of Osborne is said to have haunted the St Simons Island Lighthouse ever since the duel. Stephens said that he could regularly hear footsteps going up and down the 129 steps in the light tower, which he said was the ghost of Osborne. Twenty-seven years after the death of Osborne, in 1907, a new head keeper named Carl Svendson arrived. Svendson's tenure as head keeper of St Simons Island Lighthouse lasted almost thirty years until 1935. During a period of his tenure Svendson said that his dog had been harassed by the ghost of Osborne. Perhaps unkindly, it is said that the restless ghost of the nit-picking Frederick Osborne is checking the lighthouse on a regular basis to make sure that the light is working properly.

On the other side of the world, in Tasmania, the isolation of a lighthouse was partially held to be responsible for a lightkeeper's state of mind and subsequent behaviour although it has to be said that the behaviour could well have exhibited itself anywhere, including a large city. The introduction in the Australian Lighthouse bulletin regarding the story[11] could certainly strike a chord with most lightkeepers everywhere. The editor's note states:

> We read stories about lighthouses and imagine the romance of it all. As we investigate and talk to the lightkeepers and their families, we realise how their lives were comprised of tedious daily duties and plain hard work that revolved around keeping the light burning and maintaining the lightstations. Occasionally we are presented with tales that tell of underlying privations that reveal the harsh realities of life on the seaward edge of the civilised world.[12]

Tasmania was a harsh place for convicts and the small town of Port Arthur was the scene of a terrible massacre in 1996 when an individual named Martin Bryant went berserk and shot thirty-five people dead and wounded twenty-three others. The Tasman Island Lighthouse is one of the most remote lighthouse locations in the world, lying just over 30 miles away. It stands on Tasman Island on the south-eastern tip of the Tasman peninsula on top of windswept, storm-ravaged cliffs 1,000ft up from the sea. In common with many other lighthouses around the world, the only way on and off for many years was to be hoisted from a boat.

In early 1950 a new lightkeeper, Herbert James Yates, arrived with his girlfriend, Rita Pearl Clark, to take over the tending of the light. before he came to the lighthouse, Yates was said to be a normal young man but his character and behaviour, changed, and Yates became a different man to the person who had arrived on the island. He was known to drink heavily and became morose and aggressive towards Rita. He would regularly assault her and she lived in fear of him, a situation which was not helped by Yates having access to a rifle and knives. Despite the abuse she suffered, she stayed on the island with Yates and eventually had four children, all girls. Although she felt isolated at the lighthouse, there were three other dwellings on the island and she would seek help from the occupants on a regular basis. But nothing could be done to stop Yate's drinking and abusive behaviour towards her. Communication with the mainland from the lighthouse was restricted to flag signals from the mast at the station. It must be assumed that there were regular trips for them to be taken across to the mainland for leave and that Rita had becom accustomed to her life, unpleasant as it was. However, all that was to change with the arrival of a new ALK, eight years after Yates and his girlfriend had arrived on Tasman Island. In 1958, thirty-year-old Robert-Patrick (known as Bob) Tregenza arrived at the station to take up his duties. Bob Tregenza had been a sheep shearer, bullock driver and had served as a soldier in the Second World War before settling for a career as a lighthouse man. The new arrival was good natured with a caring personality, and it has been sugesteded[13] that Rita could not have helped being attracted to Tregenza considering the dreadful life she was leading with the appalling Yates.

Initially Tregenza and Yates worked fairly well with each other, but as time went on Tregenza could see the abuse meted out to Rita, and compassion eventually turned into a love affair between Tregenza and the long-suffering Rita. Tregenza hid the knives and took the bolt from the rifle in case Yates went into a homicidal rage. Matters finally came to a head in July 1959. On this occasion, Yates's jealousy had been growing and he had attacked Rita, almost choking her. Rushing to her aid, Tregenza knocked Yates unconscious. There appears to be some confusion over exactly what happened at this point –

whether Yates recovered and swore revenge against Tregenza and Rita but prepared to contain his rage and bide his time until the moment was right, or whether the two lovers, fearful of the maddened Yates, hid on the island until they could escape. It is said that the two men did continue working together but Yates would not allow Tregenza access to the signal flags to haul up a distress signal. However, Tregenza managed to gain access to the signal flags and hauled up the distress signal and then hid with Rita until the rescue boat came out and hoisted them to safety. It appears a peculiar set of circumstances that the maddened head keeper would be left to run the isolated lighthouse on his own in clearly a deeply unfit state of mind without immediate intervention of some kind.

Tregenza and Rita married each other shortly afterwards in Launceston and then left Tasmania with the four children (who were adopted by Tregenza) for mainland Australia, settling in Mornington, Victoria, hoping never to see Yates again.

By this time something had been done about Yates and he was under investigation. Yates had left the lighthouse service and made it his goal to track down Tregenza, Rita and his children, which he succeeded. At the couple's home in Victoria, Yates confronted Rita and said that he would kill them all, even including his own children in the murderous threat. The sad and unfortunate sequence of events continued, with Rita informing Yates that she had married Bob Tregenza which only served to drive Yates into a more murderous rage, if that were possible. Terrified for their lives, the couple and four children moved to Seaford, a suburb of Melbourne, and sought police protection. The police informed them that they could not do anything until Yates showed his hand in some way, which cannot have been any reassurance as Yates was searching nearby Frankston for them at this point. Matters may have finally resolved themselves in the family's favour, as in his crazed state of mind, Yates had given up trying to find them in their new location and attempted to commit suicide by gassing himself in Mornington. Unfortunately for the family, Yates was saved by the police and he then renewed his search for them with increased vigour. He eventually tracked the family down to their new location. On the night of 1 December 1960, Yates decided on a final showdown and just after midnight left his lodgings in Richmond with a loaded rifle and alcohol (four bottles of beer and a bottle of wine) and arrived at the family's home, bizarrely dressed in a red bow tie and dazzling white shirt. Yates had obviously spent the rest of the night drinking outside the home, because at 6 a.m. on 2 December Rita came out to go to the bakery to buy bread when she was confronted by Yates with an empty bottle of wine lying nearby. With a drunken Yates brandishing the rifle and demanding to see Tregenza, the terrified Rita turned and ran back into the house. Yates followed her and went into a bedroom to find Tregenza getting out of bed. Yates aimed the rifle at him and killed Tregenza with a single shot to the head before walking back outside the house and then shooting himself in the head. A terrified teenage girl who happened to be passing by witnessed Yates killing himself.

Bob Tregenza was buried in Coburg Cemetery, Preston, a northern suburb of Melbourne. It is a tragic story and, but for a couple of unfortunate turns, the outcome could have been very different had Tregenza and Rita managed to find safety elsewhere and if the police had not saved Yates from killing himself.

Suicides are another problem that can be associated with men who are confined for long periods, as in the case of lengthy space travel mentioned earlier. There have been very few lighthouse suicides, if only because the nature of the work and conditions is well known before it is taken on as a career. Anybody who could not take that type of life soon left of their own accord. The only known suicide in recent times, in North Ronaldsay, Scotland, was less to do with depression brought on by the isolation of the life of a lightkeeper, than the fact that he found out that his wife was involved with another man. Though unfortunate, this incident could just as easily have taken place if the lightkeeper had lived in the middle of a town and worked in a factory, though the isolation of a lighthouse may not have helped the man's state of mind.

Coming back to the situation of James Ducat, Thomas Marshall and Donald Macarthur, none of the above scenarios of murder fit the situation that the three men found themselves in on Eilean Mor. There do not appear to have been any of the problems associated with encounters with females and the jealousy arising from them. Both Ducat and Macarthur were married men whose wives were on the shore station at Breasclete. Marshall was unmarried, but any hint of problems with affairs would surely have made themselves known afterwards if foul play of any kind had been suspected. Even the violent raging arguments between Tom Howells and Tom Griffiths which took place at the Smalls Lighthouse do not appear to fit the scenario on Eilean Mor. There is a theory that one of the three men either in a fit of madness or rage went berserk, killed the other two and threw their bodies into the sea. In his madness or rage, the third man realising what he had done, then followed the other two and threw himself into the water in a fit of desperate remorse and madness. While this is certainly a possibility as there is nothing to contradict the theory, none of the circumstances seem to support such a theory. Ducat and Macarthur were both family men who by all accounts, appeared contented and basically got on with their jobs. Similarly, Thomas Marshall was a big, powerful-looking man but was considered to be a gentle giant. There was nothing in local press reports or local rumour saying that either of the men were in anyway unpleasant characters (*see* Conclusion, p. 200). However, it is certain that if there was anything untoward, it would have surfaced after the tragedy. There were unsubstantiated reports (not in the papers) that one of the three men was a drinker. Drinking of course has different effects on different people. It can make some people pleasant and amiable and it can send others into dark rages. There have been plenty of lighthousemen who drank and there are lighthousemen who have been dismissed for drinking, but it is not enough to say that one of the three men was a drinker and that somehow this led him to possibly argue with and kill his fellow workers in a fit of drunken rage and then do away with himself afterwards.

Had this scenario even been the case, it would have been expected that such a fight or the murder of his fellow lighthousemen would have taken place inside the station itself, and there would be visible signs that a violent fight had taken place (chairs turned over, tables pushed aside or crockery damaged) when Moore arrived on the station on 26 December, but as he reported, there was nothing that seemed out of place. In fact it was quite the opposite of the scene of a violent fight and murders, almost as if everything had been tidied and cleaned properly before the three men disappeared. Also if murder had taken place, it would be expected that weapons would be used, unless the other men had been incapacitated somehow. Knives or blunt objects being used would result in blood spatters and traces being left around the scene. Assuming one of the men had become deranged, after throwing the two bodies into the sea, going back into the light station to clean up the mess would not seem to be top of the priorities of someone whose mind had become unhinged, particularly as he was going to throw himself into the sea shortly afterwards. Cleaning up a murder scene to make it look as if nothing had happened is often the act of a cold and calculating murderer, but an act such as this would not be premeditated or calculated.

Leading on from MacLeod's theory of one man becoming unhinged, there is the possibility that one man ran out of the lighthouse in a highly agitated state, in this case possibly Donald Macarthur as he was in his shirtsleeves. The other two men, Ducat and Marshall, could have put on their outside clothing to protect themselves against the bad weather to go out and try and bring him back. Once outside they may have found him on the edge of a cliff or down at the west landing and in the struggle to try and restrain or calm the distraught Macarthur, they all may have fallen off the edge of the cliff into the turbulent sea or have been swept away at the west landing by a wave.

Overall, though, the theory of murder by one of the men going mad does not appear to stand up to scrutiny. A variation on this theory is that the three lightkeepers were possibly attacked by pirates or a party with murderous intentions who had landed from a passing ship. Again this is a rather far-fetched possibility. While pirates have never really gone away over the centuries, the North Atlantic area between Iceland and Scotland and Northern Ireland was not known for being an area where pirates operated. Equally, even if a passing ship had landed a party to abduct the lightkeepers, there seemed little point in doing so. There was nothing of any really value to steal and everything was in place. Even considering the very remote possibility that the three lightkeepers had been abducted for a ransom, no ransom demand was ever forthcoming. Finally, the one thing that argues against the possibility of a landing by pirates or any other malevolent party was the weather on the afternoon of 15 December 1900. From the morning the weather worsened considerably so that by the afternoon there was a strong force 9 gale blowing. There would have been 47–54mph winds and wave heights of between 23–32ft.[15] It would have been virtually impossible for a boat to have attempted to land in those conditions even if they had tried to land on the east landing.

Another possibility has been put forward[16] – that the men, or at least one or two of them, had eaten contaminated bread containing ergot. Human poisoning from eating rye bread made from ergot-contaminated grain was common in the Middle Ages. Ergot itself is a group of fungi of which the most prominent member is rye ergot fungus (*Claviceps purpurea*). It grows on rye and plants related to rye and produces alkaloids that cause ergotism in humans and mammals that eat grains which have been contaminated with its fruiting structure. Although rye is the most common host and therefore the most affected, the contamination can also take place in wheat barley and triticale (a hybrid of wheat and rye that was first developed in laboratories in the late nineteenth century), although oats are rarely affected.

The ergot kernel is known as the sclerotium, and this kernel contains a high level (up to 2 per cent of the dry mass) of an alkaloid known as ergotamine. Whilst the full description and effects of the alkaloid might appear to require a chemistry degree to understand it, suffice to say that from a layman's point of view, the alkaloid ergotamine has a link to lysergic acid through the way it is biosynthesised by the fungus. While it is connected to lysergic acid, it is not actual LSD (lysergic acid diethylamide). It contains ergotamine which is used to synthesize lysergic acid which is a precursor for synthesizing LSD itself. Eating bread contaminated by ergot can have a number of effects on humans including the neurotransmission and circulatory systems. Severe pathological syndromes can also affect humans once they have ingested the bread. It can lead to hallucinations, extremely irrational behaviour, convulsions and death. Other symptoms include strong uterine contractions, nausea, seizures and unconsciousness. It has had a long history stretching from the Middle Ages and was also known as St Anthony's Fire due to the burning sensation in the limbs felt by sufferers, caused by severe constriction of the blood vessels. In some cases it leads to gangrene and complete loss of limbs. St Anthony's Fire also refers to the Hospital Order of St Anthony, an order of monks established in 1095 who specialised in treating victims of ergotism. One of the most peculiar properties of such a deadly fungus is that it was used to also treat some illnesses. Ergot extract has been used in some pharmaceutical products to treat migraine headaches and also to induce uterine contractions in pregnant women, as well as controlling bleeding after childbirth. The use of ergot to induce abortion and control bleeding after childbirth was fairly common in the Middle Ages. Such a volatile drug can have its own problems. A study of 11,000 patients who had Parkinson's disease and were being treated with ergot-derived drugs found that they increased the risk of leaky heart valves by up to 700 per cent.[17]

One example of hysteria that may have been induced by ergot is the Salem Witch Trials in Massachusetts in 1692–1693, this theory was put forward by Linnda Caporael in 1976, although the idea has been disputed.

A second example is the legend of the Pied Piper of Hamelin, the roots of which are possibly based in fact. Hamelin (Hameln) is a town in Lower Saxony, Germany, where in 1284 the town's children died or were lured away by the music of a piper who wore multi-coloured clothing. In the sixteenth century the legend was given a fuller narrative, with the piper saying to the mayor of Hamelin that he will rid the town of their plague of rats for the payment of a set price per rat. Using his pipe the piper entranced the rats, which followed him out of the town and into the River Weser where all but one drowned. The Pied Piper felt he had kept his side of the bargain and went back to claim his payment. When the mayor refused to pay him the full amount as he had agreed, the piper swore revenge. On St John and Paul's Day, the piper returned while all the townspeople were in church and started playing music on his pipe, using his magic to lure the town's children (130 of them) away. The children willingly followed him and danced along as they followed the mysterious piper out of Hamelin never to be seen again. Only three children were left behind: one blind child who could not see where he was going, one lame child who could not keep up with the others and one child who was deaf and could not hear the music. These three children told the townspeople what had happened when they came out of church. There are various other endings to the tale, which include the children being taken into the River Weser and drowning, as had happened to the rats. Another version has the Pied Piper returning the children after receiving payment in full – a variation on this is that the children are only returned after the full payment is made to him many times over in gold.[18]

With regards to the actual roots of the tale, there are several theories. One is that the children died of natural causes such as an epidemic of disease or an accident – The tale is often consdered a variation on the *Danse Macabre* or 'Dance of Death'. Another theory has the story as an allegory for the emigration, with the 'children' being unemployed and moving away to colonies in Eastern Europe to work. Other theories have the children leaving on pilgrimages or military campaigns. Yet another theory has the Pied Piper portrayed as a psychopathic paedophile.[19]

One often mooted theory[20] is that the consumption of ergot-tainted rye bread is responsible and in dancing after the piper (who is an allegorical figure in this case – that is, death itself) the children literally danced themselves to exhaustion and death. Something that was known to happen during the Middle Ages.

So going back to the Flannan Islands in December 1900, would it have been possible that one or more of the men had consumed ergot-tainted bread and then gone mad as a result? It is of course a possibility but it has to be considered what their behaviour would have been like had they done so. The erratic and spasmodic behaviour in a hallucinating state would have made the men careless about what they were doing. From the Muirhead and Moore's reports, the implication is that the men appeared to have all been working normally right up to the moment they all disappeared, with cooking utensils all washed and put away and the work of the lighthouse done, all ready for the light to be started once it got dark on the evening of 15 December 1900. The possibility that one went mad from the ergot and then rushed out and pushed the other two over a cliff and then followed them over is another scenario. The occasional keeper, Donald Macarthur, was in his shirtsleeves, but one can possibly draw the conclusion that he was duty cook for that week and may have been about to start preparing for the next meal while Ducat and Marshall went out in their weatherproof gear. Even if Macarthur had gone mad from eating ergot and rushed outside to attack the other two at the west landing, he would have had to overpower two men in very awkward conditions as there was little space for a struggle to take place once the lightkeepers had gone any way down the steps. However, the two men could have been taken completely by surprise and during a struggle all three may have fallen down the cliff and into the water. There were railings for safety but there is no way of knowing if these had been torn away by the force of the water (as stated in Muirhead's report) at the time any possible struggle may have taken place, or whether this happened afterwards.

The balance of probability is that it is most unlikely ergot-tainted bread had been involved. All the evidence seems to point to the supposition that whatever happened to the men, it occurred in the course of their work. The tidy appearance of the station, with everything in order, plus the donning of sea boots and oilskins by two of the men shows they were paying attention to their surroundings. In the absence of any other evidence to support it, this theory can be largely discounted.

To a modern-day researcher, it would seem that one of the oddest aspects of the tragedy is that basically only one man investigated what had happened, meaning that only one official was tasked with the responsibility in any official capacity.

Ducat, Marshall and Macarthur were essentially public servants who disappeared while on duty and presumed dead. Yet there was absolutely no police involvement and not one policeman set foot on the island; it is inconceivable that three men would disappear at work today without the police investigating it. It can be argued that the police know nothing about lightkeeping or the workings of a lighthouse. The likelihood that one of the men murdered the other two and then did away with himself is slim; yet there was some possibility of foul play and the police appear to have been content for the NLB to investigate the incident themselves nonetheless. It would seem that no working party or committee of relevant individuals who could give some input in the investiagtion – such as a master mariner, a policeman, a senior individual from Trinity House and a senior member of the legal profession – was formed. The whole incident, from start to finish, was left to Robert Muirhead to investigate and report on. There is no doubt that Muirhead did his very best and that he would have devoted some considerable time and effort to investigating the tragedy. However, he was still acting as superintendent and expected to get on with his normal job at the same time, for instance seeing that NLB Secretary James Murdoch's instructions were carried out for the immediate restarting of the Eilean Mor Light. He does not appear to have been able to step back from his normal function and solely concentrate on the investigation, although in fairness, there is no doubt that his attention would have been focused on what had happened on the Flannans from the day of the discovery on 26 December 1900 through to the production of his report on the 8 January 1901.

Equally, the legal profession appear to have been content to take a hands-off approach. Members of the Scottish legal profession have regularly served as NLB commissioners, including the Lord Advocate, so there was direct involvement in the running of the NLB by Scottish lawyers. Initially it was felt that a full inquiry might have been necessary; however, on 1 February 1901 the Crown Office in Edinburgh sent a letter to NLB Secretary James Murdoch. The letter was headed 'Flannans Disaster' and stated:

Sir,
Referring to my letter 29th ulto, I am desired by Crown Counsel to inform you that the question raised by your letter of the 22nd ulto has been considered by them, and that they have come to the conclusion, contrary to their previous opinion, that it is not necessary to hold an inquiry under the Act of 1895. I am further desired to ask you to be good enough to send me, for the perusal of Crown Counsel, the Report which your board have already obtained, from your Officer, as to the accident, with relative documents.

I am Sir
Your Obedient Servant
NJ Douglas
Crown Agent[21]

The decision had already been made, therefore, that a formal inquiry would not be necessary *without* even seeing Muirhead's report. The relative documents being requested to be sent to them for perusal with Muirhead's report would most likely include witness statements[22] taken by Muirhead, but would almost certainly include the station logbook, possibly the station scrapbook and any other official and unofficial paperwork Muirhead may have found and brought back with him to Edinburgh.

The attitude by the police and legal profession may have been more understandable had the three men's bodies been found or washed ashore and it could have been proven that they died from drowning, which would have appeared a straightforward case of misadventure. However, there was no definitive proof of that, despite the circumstantial evidence of damage to the west landing.

The NLB obviously had the utmost confidence in Robert Muirhead to do a satisfactory job with his investigation. In the wake of the tragedy, Muirhead, along with members of the tender's crew and the replacement keepers, were the only people who set foot on Eilean Mor; there appears to be no record of anyone else doing so. Even so, the almost casual approach to the disappearances by the other authorities does seem rather puzzling, under the circumstances.

Notes
1 I am indebted to Merrilyn Macaulay and Donnie G. Macleod, the son of Donald John MacLeod, for this account. See also webonetel.net.uk/~breasclete/CEKeeper.html.
2 Ibid.
3 Ibid.

4 Dr Jay C. Buckey Jr is a former astronaut and has extensively researched psychological issues in relation to space travel.
5 *Scottish Islands Explorer* magazine, May/June 2013 issue.
6 I am very grateful to David R. Collin for his kind permission to use the description of his account on that day.
7 The link to David R. Collin's account of the murder is on www.kirkcudbright.com.
8 I am very grateful to Sheila Ryan for her kind permission to use her account of this case based on her research. Her website is www.sheila-ryan.co.uk.
9 See www.trinityhouse.co.uk/lighthouses/lighthouse_list/smalls.html.
10 See en.wikipedia.org/wiki/St._Simons_Island_Light.
11 'Tasman is Murder', www.lighthouse.net.au, bulletin no. 6 2003. The original account of the Tasman Island story first appeared in the *Melbourne Truth* newspaper.
12 Ibid.
13 Ibid.
14 Ibid.
15 Meteorological Office Archives Exeter – see Appendix III.
16 There are numerous examples on the Internet of how ergot has possibly been involved in famous events such as the Salem Witch Trials or the Pied Piper of Hamelin. See for instance www.jimcofer.com blog.
17 *New England Journal of Medicine*, 4 January 2007.
18 See en.wikipedia.org/wiki/Pied_piper.
19 The psychopathic paedophile theory proposed by William Manchester in *A World Lit Only By Fire*, Little, Brown & Co., 1992.
20 Searching on the Internet for the Pied Piper of Hamelin and ergot will bring up a number of references where the theory is discussed or presented.
21 Crown Office Crown Counsel correspondence, Scottish National Archive file nos NLC2/1/88, NLC2/1/89.
22 There were, of course, no witnesses to the disappearance. This simply refers to formal statements taken by anyone connected with the station and the arrival of the *Hesperus*.

8

SUPERNATURAL

An idea of the nature of how the islands were viewed by the more learned members of the inhabitants of the Scottish Highlands and islands is given by the Scottish writer, Martin Martin. He was a native of Bealach, near Duntulm on Skye and had graduated from Edinburgh University with an MA in 1681. He wrote a book entitled *A Description of the Western Islands of Scotland*,[1] which was originally published in 1695. This description of the Isles in particular, despite its age, has become the main reference work for all other books which followed to date. Samuel Johnson and James Boswell took a copy of the corrected second edition (1703) on their tour of the Hebrides in Autumn 1773. A good explanation of the early travellers' accounts is given in an excellent work[2] by Martin Rackwitz, who refers to all accounts by the travellers in the Highlands and Hebrides between 1600 and 1800.

With the folklore and superstitions of the Western Isles and no trace whatsoever of the three men being found, it was inevitable a supernatural explanation of some kind would be sought. In addition to this was the nature of the lighthouse living quarters when the *Hesperus* arrived with the relief – the empty rooms, the fire gone out, all the clocks stopped, the light itself not working – which provided an eerie aspect to the tale, as if the men had been there one minute and vanished into thin air the next. It was also inevitable that parallels would be drawn with the *Mary Celeste*.[3] The 'uneaten meal' and the 'overturned chair' supposedly found at the Flannans Lighthouse, which in fact first appeared the poem *Flannan Isle* by Wilfrid Wilson Gibson. are redolent of the often misreported account of the 'uneaten breakfast' and 'still warm tea' on the table found on the *Mary Celeste* when she was boarded after being found drifting 600 miles west of Portugal, It is certainly possible that the inspiration for this part of the poem came to Gibson from the story of the *Mary Celeste*. Gibson was a Georgian poet, born in Hexham, Northumberland in 1878, who became a good friend of Rupert Brooke. Gibson had been a social worker in London's East End and had served on the front line in the First World War. His poems, understandably, tended to concern themselves with poverty and the life of a soldier at war. His poem on the Flannan Isle disaster (*see* Appendix I) is written in the macabre style which he used for some of his poetry. Although Gibson's work was popular, it was often overshadowed by that of Ezra Pound, of the T.S. Eliot School of modernist poetry.

There have been a number of other literary references to the Flannans tragedy, most with little of substance to add to the story. One particular account[4] centres on Joseph Moore and his experience with mysterious birds when entering the lighthouse. It is a well-written account, although there are a number of factual inaccuracies. For instance, the height of the light tower at 275ft is incorrect, corresponding neither to the height of the tower itself nor its total height above sea level. The account states that while he was on leave ashore at Breasclete, Moore looked across with horror at Eilean Mor from Lewis to see only blackness. Where this has come from is not known, as it is certainly not mentioned anywhere in the documents held by the Scottish National Archive. This was supposedly five days before he was due to travel out to the lighthouse after his leave. It further states that Moore wanted to travel out immediately but was stopped from doing so by gales. The first official intimation in the archive records that anything was wrong was the arrival of the *Hesperus* on 26 December – there is no doubt that a sense of foreboding must have arisen when there was no response to the rocket and ship's horn blast from the *Hesperus* as it approached the island, but there is no hint of real worry before this.

Perhaps the most interesting aspect of this account concerned three birds. It was a story told among locals on Lewis that when Joseph Moore opened the door and went into the Eilean Mor Lighthouse for the first time on 26 December 1900, three giant, black birds that were on top of the light tower, flew away from the lighthouse and out to sea. It was felt that these were the bodies of Ducat, Marshall and Macarthur which had turned into birds, the reasoning being that the men had transgressed the sanctity of the island and this was their punishment. At the time it is possible that superstition could have argued this away, as the men represented the first official permanent habitation on the island; earlier visitors (farmers and sheep herders and religious folk) had been of a transient nature. Of course there were labourers on the island building the station for the best part of almost four years and the lighthouse had already been in operation for a year without any problems. Whilst it can be said that Moore made no mention of the three large, black birds in his report, on his eventual return to Breasclete some weeks later, before his next posting, it is quite possible that Moore may have repeated the story to people there. It should be remembered that Joseph Moore, by his own admission, was deeply unhappy about being posted onto the island after the tragedy, despite being on the roster for the station at that time. NLB Superintendent Robert Muirhead was also deeply concerned about Moore's mental state and resolved to move him as soon as the replacements had settled in.[5] Whilst Moore had said to Muirhead that he was very unhappy about having to stay on Eilean Mor, and he had written his report on what he found that day at the deserted station, he would be unlikely to have written about three large black birds flying off the light tower and out to sea, knowing how such an account might be received by the sober Lighthouse Commissioners in Edinburgh. Neither was Moore left alone for two days to await relief in the lighthouse on 26 December – as stated in the account, he was accompanied. The telegram from Captain Harvey of the *Hesperus* announcing the disaster to NLB Secretary James Murdoch said: 'I have left Moore, MacDonald, Buoymaster, and two seamen on the Island to keep the light burning until you make other arrangements.'[6]

Overall, this version is a good short account of the tragedy and, like Martin Martin, hints at the superstitions people had, believing the island contained a malevolent force. However, it finishes with a statement that, as an explanation of the disappearance of the three men, the three birds account does stretch the imagination.

There is another account of similar events which hints at supernatural involvement.[7] The section dealing with the Flannan Isles concerns itself more with the legends and folklore of the Isle of Lewis and the Flannans. Centring on the stones at Callanish (here named Callernish), the section describes the stones as the Great Stone Circle of the Serpent and Winged Disc. An atmospheric description of Callanish is given of the light never quite fading at midnight, along with a comparison of the stones and the nearby sea being similar in many ways to the Cyclopian legends of the Greek Islands. As a stone temple, Callanish is described as being unusual in having no hill or mound associated with it. The account states that sacrifices were made on Callanish and that the Flannan Isles was the place where the bodies were taken to be received by the Gods. Reference is also made to Martin Martin's view of the superstitions and language of the area. The other name for the Flannan Isles, the Seven Hunters, is given as having magical connotations and compares them to the seven islands of Wak in the *Arabian Nights* story, where the hero Hasan goes in search of his swan-maiden bride. There is also reference to the stone chapel on Eilean Mor and the fact that it is not precisely known who built it. The account further states that the existence of the chapel heightens the sense of sanctity of the place and that the Flannan Isles, in common with other places such as Heligoland and the Scilly Isles, were places where the dead were taken. The problem of ships and the rocks at the Flannans is then mentioned, along with the construction of the lighthouse itself, and a description of Ducat, Marshall and Macarthur's disappearance. There are some inaccuracies in the account, such as the description of the weather between 14 and 19 December as calm.[8]

Coming back to the idea of sacrifices, the account mentions that at the time of the disappearance of the three lightkeepers, sacrifices were still being carried out at Loch Maree and probably in other remote parts of the Highlands. The idea of human sacrifice in towers to the Gods or supernatural beings had a parallel in the 1973 film *Wicker Man*. In the film, which is set (but not filmed) in the Hebrides, a policeman (played by Edward Woodward) searching for a missing girl on the island finds that a kind of Celtic paganism is practised by the inhabitants. At the end of the film, Woodward's policeman is sacrificed, along with animals, in a giant wicker man, as an offering to the Gods due to a crop failure.[9]

The reputation of the Flannan Isles as a haunt of spirits is mentioned in connection with the story of John Morison, who was marooned on Eilean Mor in the seventeenth century. The fire he had lit had gone out and with no means of relighting it Morison was starting to get worried, as he was sure to perish without heat. He was then confronted by a man who told him there was fire on an altar in the chapel. Morison was able to use this to keep his fire going until help came to get him off the island.[10]

One of the main points made in this account[11] is that a supernatural race of small aboriginal people were believed to inhabit the islands west of Lewis. An early traveller named Donald Munro had seen some of the bones of this race of pigmy-type people being dug out of the earth, including a skull. It states that there was much dislike and even hatred between the early Christians of the Isles and these people.

The story of this race of small people could have its origins in the Scottish 'Kelpie' water sprites that were said to inhabit stretches of sea, rivers and lochs. One type of Kelpie were called the Blue Men of the Minch, or Storm Kelpies, and were said to occupy the sea between Lewis and the mainland of Scotland looking for sailors to drown and boats in distress to sink.[12] Mention is also made of the hostility between the pigmies and Christians resulting in the hanging of St Frangus on top of a hill (*see* p.184). An account is also given of a local woman, who lived on Great Bernera (a small island between Lewis and the Flannan Islands) who had spent a night with the little people when she was four years old. The little people had looked after her and played music all night before returning her safe and sound to her home. Further on it states that the human offerings were ferried out to Eilean Mor and that this practice was stopped with the coming of Christianity, and simultaneous with the arrival of Christianity was the disappearance of the little men. The account then says that the disappearance of the Flannan Islands lightkeepers is an extension of an extraordinary age-old ritual of sacrifice, whereby the men were taken from Long Island near Callernish and taken over to the Island of the Dead, Eilean Mor, where they were installed in a tower, similar to those once used for human sacrifice, and taken by the Gods. It gives an example of one on the opposite coast at Dun Carloway. The parallel is that the lighthousemen went over to the Flannan Isles and were installed in a tower (the lighthouse itself) and then disappeared.[13]

Yet another account[14] discusses the lightkeepers' disappearance as being due to their presence on the island as offending 'Sky Folk'. Eilean Mor is described as being an ancient haunted place and also a place where bodies said to be 'unholy' were taken for ritual internment. The small chapel on the island was said to guard the remains of the dead. The building of a large and modern lighthouse which reached into the sky disturbed the sanctity of the island and the lightkeepers paid the price. Joseph Moore again comes into this account when it was said that he had boarded the *Hesperus* to travel out to the island but that he was delayed as the weather changed violently within that day and he had to wait for one further day. Oddly, this account mentions the irregularity of the cloth (blinds) not being drawn during daylight, something which Muirhead made no mention of in his report and something which he surely would have made a note of as an obvious irregularity. The account also goes into some detail about the 'dramatic entries' in the log book (*see* Chapter 4). The conclusion drawn from this account is that the men were aware of their impending doom and prayed towards the end before their complete disappearance for offending the 'Sky Folk'.[15]

The theme of abduction (including alien abduction) of the three lightkeepers is also present in other accounts.[16] There are also many accounts of the small race of men who occupied the islands.

In the early 1900s, writer W.C. MacKenzie wrote an article on the 'Pigmie Isle' at the Butt of Lewis and the Pygmies' chapel there. He mentioned that the first traveller who had visited the 'Pigmie Isle' in a pastoral capacity and wrote of his visit was clergyman Donald Monro (known as Dean of the Isles). Monro visited the Islands in 1563 and wrote a manuscript of his visit entitled *A Description of the Western Isles of Scotland*, which was not published until 1582 and was only made available to the wider public in 1774. He wrote in his manuscript that he went to the north point of Lewis and visited:

> a little Isle called the 'Pigmies Isle' with a little kirk in it of their own handiwork. Within this kirk the ancients of that country of the Lewis say that the said pigmies have been buried there. Many men of different countries have delved deeply the floor of the little kirk, and I myself among the rest, and have found in it, deep under the earth, certain bones and round heads of wonderful little size, alleged to be

the bones of the said pigmies; which may be likely, according to sundry histories that we read of the pigmies; but I leave this far to the ancients of Lewis.[17]

This description of Monro's is used by the sixteenth-century scholar George Buchanan in his *History of Scotland*. Further reference was made to the Pigmies' kirk and the bones in an official account of Lewis which was written in 1580. It stated the pigmies' bones were measured and found to be not quite 2in long.

Another description of the Pigmies Isle was given by Captain John Dymes, who visited the Isle in 1630. He too dug up some of the pigmies' bones, but he expressed some scepticism, stating: 'My belief is scarce big enough to think them to be human bones.'[18] John Morison, who was a Lewisman himself, also expressed scepticism. Despite Morison having written about being confronted by a supernatural being when his fire was in danger of going out on Eilean Mor (*see* p. 175), he dismisses the idea of the bones being human in an account he wrote of Lewis and the islands in 1680. He believed the bones to be those of small fowl.

The authoritative account of the Western Isles by Martin Martin also refers to the small bones which had been dug up. He stated: 'This gave ground to a tradition which the natives have, of a very low-statured people living once here, called 'lusbirdan' or pigmies.'[19]

The word lusbirdan is considered to equate to the modern word *luspardan*, which, both in Gaelic and Scots, means pigmy. There were a number of variations of the word with the Gaelic academic Dr Alexander MacBain believing the word (included in his dictionary) to be derived from *lugh-spiorad*, or 'little spirit', though other scholars give the word other derivations, including as the Rev. John Jamieson in his dictionary of the Scottish language.

In a map drawn by Dutch cartographer Willem Blaeu, the name of the Isle is given as Ylen Dunibeg, or Island of the Little Men. A visitor to the isle in 1630, Captain John Dymes, drew a rough sketch of Lewis and on this map the isle is described as the Isle of Pigmies. The same name is also used by Martin Martin although he states in his book that the natives of the area (like Blaeu) described it as the 'Island of Little Men,' a distinction with a slight difference. In the earliest Ordnance Survey maps, the Isle appears as Luchruban, which is almost identical with Luchorpain, or Luchrupain, who were diminutive people of Irish legend. The full name of the Isle was probably Eilean na Luchrupáin, or Island of the Luchrupain, the dwarfs who were complementary to the Irish Fomhoraiqh (Fomorians) or giants. It is not known when this name supplanted that of the 'Pigmie Isle', but not improbably, it was given to the Isle by Irish antiquaries, who thought they had discovered in the small bones, relics of their legendary race of small men known as Luchrupdin. Captain Dymes believed that the bones had often been dug up, especially by the Irish who came to the area for that purpose. The context seems to show that he meant natives of Ireland, and not merely Gaelic speakers.

There is occasionally confusion as to where the pigmies lived on Lewis and the exact location of the 'Pigmie Isle' itself. Sometimes the 'Pigmie Isle' is taken to mean Eilean Mor itself, but this is not the case.

In his detailed article[20] on the 'Pigmie Isle', William Cook MacKenzie found that the most recent reference to it was in an ode published in 1749 by the poet William Collins, entitled 'An Ode on the Popular Superstitions of the Highlands of Scotland'. Collins had been a firm believer in the 'Pigmie Isle' and the folklore that went with it.

There were sceptics of the idea of little people inhabiting any part of Lewis, however. In addition to John Morison's dismissal of the bones as wild fowl in 1680, Dr John McCulloch published his *Highlands and Islands* handbook in 1877. In the handbook McCulloch disputed that any such Pigmie Isle actually ever existed and also criticised George Buchanan's account of it in his *History of Scotland* (Buchanan had relied on Dean Monro's account for his version). In his article, W.C. Mackenzie felt that McCulloch's dismissal of the 'Pigmie Isle', and thus Monro's reputation, had been called into question, he. Mackenzie therefore felt duty bound to restore Monro's reputation as a reliable witness and writer.

Mackenzie, along with his brother C.G. MacKenzie and his cousin Dr Mackenzie, set about trying to find the Isle of Pigmies themselves. As a starting point they used the description of the Isle given in the manuscript of Captain Dymes which had originally been written in 1630. As mentioned previously, Captain Dymes had drawn a map, which made locating the isle easier. W.C. MacKenzie himself was not physically involved in the search. He left this to his brother and cousin to carry out because they both lived nearby in Stornoway. The map drawn by Captain Dymes aided them greatly and they were able to find both the Pigmie Isle and the chapel. The isle lay to the north-west of the lighthouse at the Butt of Lewis and had a length of roughly 80ft and a width of roughly 70ft. It was cut off from the Isle of Lewis by very high tides. A conspicuous feature of the landscape of the island was the short, deep-green seagrass that covered the surface.

Despite their obvious delight at finding the isle and chapel, the hope of finding any direct link to the pigmies themselves was disappointing. Dr Mackenzie drew up a list of their discoveries but these were handmade glazed and unglazed pottery, some bones and a small quantity of peat ash. With their disappointment over the lack of evidence of pigmies, they nevertheless felt that the chapel was of some relevance as it was purported to have been used by them. Dr MacKenzie described the visible part of the structure which he had seen as follows:

> I found only the oblong portion, partially exposed to view. The walls of this portion are composed of flat and neatly-laid stones, unmortared. They are 2 feet in thickness, and stand from their foundations at a general height of 2 feet.

About the middle of the south wall, there is a shallow opening, 18 inches wide, forming part of the two sides and bottom of a square. It appears to have been used as a window. Its sill is 18 inches from the foundation line of the walls.[21]

The visible portion of the structure found by Dr MacKenzie was the same part which had been seen by Monro in 1549 and by later enquirers. Dr Mackenzie, like the earlier visitors, dug up the floor of the chapel. He found bones and patterned pottery which lay between the upper layer of loam and the lower layer of sea-sand. The pottery consisted of:

one piece of the bottom, with part of the side, of a small vessel of reddish clay, not made on the wheel or fired in a kiln, and unglazed; three portions apparently of the sides of different vessels of dark micaceous clay, about ¼ inch in thickness, somewhat resembling the old craggans, and ornamented with rough parallel scratches, as if drawn with the broken end of a twig; and a fourth fragment, showing the lip of a larger vessel, elegantly shaped, well smoothed on the inside, and the outside ornamented with the same linear striation. The loam at both ends of the layer was impregnated with a reddish material, resembling damp peat-ashes.[22]

Dr Mackenzie went on to describe the details of part of the structure – a passage, 21in wide, which led due west from the kirk (actually described as the 'so-called Kirk') for a distance of 6½ft. Its walls, which were 2ft high, were dry-built and plumb. There were two interruptions in the wall, one on the south side, where it should have abutted on the west end of the chapel, and the other on the opposite side. The former, which had a width of 27in, appears to have been the doorway of the structure. The niche on the north side was semi-circular in shape; it was 41in wide and had an extreme depth of 30in. The floor of carefully laid flat stones was about

9in above the general level of the passage floor. The roof of this recess appeared to have been semi-circular in shape. At the western end, the passage opened into a roofless circular apartment which was about 10ft in diameter. Its walls were very well built of dry stone, which rose from the foundations to a height of about 4ft. At the west of the chamber, peat ash was found, and under the floor some more of the small bones. In the wall of this chamber was a small square recess 17in high, 15in broad, and 19in deep. The interior of the entire structure (which comprised the circular chamber, the passage, and the kirk) measured 24ft 9in. There was a slope on the floor from the western to the eastern end, the gradient estimated to be around 1 in 50. One feature of the circular apartment and the passage was the drainage system, which was still present at the time Dr MacKenzie made his excavations at the chapel. A carefully built drain made up of flat stones laid in a 'V' shape entered under the foundations. From this point, the drainage ran in front of the fireplace in the circular chamber where the ashes were found, and curved under the full width of the floor through the passage. Opposite the niche in the passage, it was joined by another drain of the same construction, which emerged from the floor of the niche. From this junction, it passed to the outside through the doorway, not apparently having entered the kirk at all. The contents of the drain, a dark-coloured deposit, were freely dotted with a pure white substance resembling chloride of lime.

The whole structure of the chapel was surrounded by what appeared to have been an old turf-grown stone dyke. The diameter of the enclosure measured approximately 40ft. This dyke impinged upon the building at its west end, came close to both the chapel and the edge of the cliff on the south and east sides and was furthest from it on the north-west side.

Once he had finished his work of measuring and digging, Dr Mackenzie believed that the character of the whole structure had, for the first time, been revealed by the excavations. Dr MacKenzie had also travelled to Eilean Mor on the Flannan

Isles in 1896 and he felt that the roofs of the chambers and the passage between them and the pigmies chapel (which had gone by the time of his visit), were probably similar to those of the stone buildings he had seen on Eilean Mor. The buildings on Eilean Mor consisted of large slabs of stone forming a beehive dome, with a circular hole at or near the apex, while the passages were lintelled over with flat slabs. There was a possibility that turf was used to cover the structure for security and concealment.

W.C. MacKenzie felt that the structure his cousin and brother had unearthed was unique, although some of the general primitive structures found in the Hebrides could be loosely classified with it. What set it apart from anything else, he felt, was the oblong chamber being used as a kirk or chapel. He felt it was too small to be used for this purpose, although it was possible it could have been used as the oratory of a hermit who made the circular chamber his dwelling. Neither did he believe that one chamber had been added to the other, surmising that the dwelling as it stood was clearly the original design. Dr MacKenzie stated that the chapel on Eilean Mor had a similar plan and that it stood apart from the beehive buildings there – its wall structure was the same, but its dimensions were slightly smaller than the pigmies chapel on the Butt of Lewis. W.C. Mackenzie had given what might seem to be a rather lengthy and over-elaborate description of the pigmies chapel. He also attempted to distance himself somewhat by saying in his article about the chapel: 'It will be remembered that Dean Monro declared it was the handiwork of the pigmies themselves.'[23]

However, there is little doubt that he was delighted they had found the chapel, and whether or not it had originally been built by the pigmies, William Cook Mackenzie had proved to the wider world that such a chapel actually existed, even if no pigmy bones had been unearthed.

One of the local pieces of folklore concerns an outlaw by the name of St Frangus. Quite how he achieves the status of an outlaw and that of a saint at the same time is unexplained. Saint Frangus was said to live at Ness on the sands of Lionel. The tale concerns St Frangus and the pigmies of Luchruban and is believed to have been passed down by word of mouth, with one of the oldest residents of Ness relating the tale. Apparently St Frangus did not get on with the pigmies and was unkind to them. In what form the unkindness was displayed is unexplained, but it was bad enough for the pigmies to hang him on a hill, which was then named Bruich Frangus. It is believed that St Frangus may have used the structure at Luchruban as a place of retreat, which would account for the naming of the smaller chamber as a 'chapel.' However, there were the remains of other chapels and oratories along the coast of Lewis and in the numerous inlets, and the structure at Luchruban resembled them somewhat, so it probably became known as a chapel on account of that similarity.

Ethnological research in the early twentieth century had shown that the origins of the 'pigmies' were not entirely certain, but they were believed to have been Spaniards, who came to Lewis around 500 years BC. In the year AD 1 'big yellow men' were believed to have arrived from Argyll and driven the pigmies from Cunndal (a cove near Luchruban) to the island of Luchruban. The pigmies grew in number over a period of time and then emigrated to Europe and Knockaird in the same vicinity. It is said that they lived on 'buffaloes' (presumably oxen), which they killed by throwing 'sharp-pointed knives' at them. The folklore generally tallies with the ethnological research that the small, dark aborigines were invaded by the Goidels or early Celts. At Cunndal, W.C. Mackenzie discovered some twenty-five hut circles, with one of them having stone foundations and the others being simply mounds of turf. Mackenzie could find no information in the district about the hut-circles, except that they had been used for storing seaweed and for fish-curing purposes. However, further inquiries by him found that the hut circles had stood there 'from time immemorial', and, according to an old Ness man, they had formed the dwellings of his pigmies prior to their migration to Luchruban.

There was some dispute as to how the legend of the pigmies came about, with both John Morison and Martin Martin believing that the legend arose as a result of the discovery of the small bones at Luchruban. Dean Monro, however, believed that the legend was independent of the discovery of the small bones, and other observers were of the same opinion. The question of the origin of the small bones was partly laid to rest by W.C. Mackenzie, who decided to have them examined by an expert. He arranged for them to be sent to the Natural History Museum at South Kensington where they were examined by anatomist Dr Charles W. Andrews. Dr Andrews examined the bones in great detail and found them not to be human: Of the fourteen samples sent to him, seven of them were the bones of mammals and seven were those of birds. The mammals comprised oxen, young lambs, sheep, and a dog (or a fox); the birds were classified as rock pigeon, the razorbill, the greater and the lesser black-backed gull, and possibly a petrel (difficult to classify due to the bone being a portion of a mandible). From this investigation it was deduced that mammals and birds formed the diet of the dwellers in this area. With the exception of the ox, the animals and birds represented by the bones were all indigenous to the district, and even in MacKenzie's time gulls were largely used for human food at Ness.

Although Mackenzie felt that he had laid to rest the theory of the existence of pigmies, he also felt that, despite a large part of the legend being tied to the bones in the structure at Luchruban, allowance had to be made for the exaggeration of tradition and folklore which 'measured its low-statured peoples by inches, just as it measures its tall peoples by yards.' From this observation he stated 'we have pigmies and giants to represent races who were shorter or taller than the race perpetuating the traditions'. The folklore of the area seems to have grown up around the existence of the pigmies, completely separate to the discovery of the small bones which were used to bolster the legends.

Mackenzie said that it appeared to be fairly obvious that:

> the pigmies of Luchruban were simply a prehistoric people of short stature and dark hair, who were contemptuously called Danibeg or 'little men' by their successors, a name which was inaccurately Englished and perpetuated as 'pigmies'. Naturally, the discovery of the small bones would give a tremendous fillip to the pigmy idea, and so the error persisted owing to the ignorance of comparative anatomy which prevailed. It is at least satisfactory to have given this myth a final burial.[24]

He went on to say that the Isle of Lewis offered a remarkably rich field of investigation to the ethnologist, in view of the marked diversity of the types on the island. The prominent Victorian ethnologist Dr John Beddoe, suggested that one of the types was 'a short, thick-set, snub-nosed, dark-haired, and even dark-eyed race', and that it was more than likely aboriginal and possibly even Finnish in origin. It was possible that Laplanders or Finns have some physical affinities with the shorter and darker type of Lewisman (a type which in Mackenzie's time were sparsely represented in the island), while the qammar or huts of the Lapps, as described by travellers, bear a resemblance to the Luchruban structure as it must have been originally designed. There were also (remarked by W.C. Mackenzie) customs which lingered in Lewis as recently as the eighteenth, or even the nineteenth century, which have elsewhere been regarded as peculiar to Lapland.

The Swedish zoologist and archaeologist, Professor Sven Nilssen, carried out research which showed that the pigmies of tradition and the dwarfs of the Sagas belonged to the same race as the Laplanders of the present day. Moreover, the well-authenticated traditions in Shetland about the Finn-men apparently offer corroboration of the view that the 'little men' of these islands were of Finnish or Lapponic origin. The Firbolg were a race of short, dark men in Irish mythology, who were driven from Ireland to the Hebrides by the Tuatha de Danaan and were also believed to represent the same race of pigmies. The Firbolg were also thought to have been the first inhabitants of St Kilda.

W.C. Mackenzie concluded that while Highland folk-lore was full of the Famhuirean (the Irish Fomorians) or giants, he observed that there was a curious absence of the complementary Luchrupain or dwarfs and wondered how this could be accounted for? His belief was that they were represented by the fairies (our old friends as he described them), who were sometimes called Daoine Beaqa, also the ancient name of the Pigmies Isle. It was a bit of a stretch to make the connections that Mackenzie was suggesting. However he was to make one more concerning the Lewis fairies. One of their names is Muinntir Fionnlagh, often translated as the Finlay people, a title which, as applied to fairies, has baffled scholars of Lewis folklore. He suggested that this name meant 'the little Finn people', and that it linked the Finnish aborigines with the 'good little people' of fairy lore who dwelt in the bowels of green hills like Luchruban.[25]

The subject of the missing lightkeepers having become prey to some malevolent force or creature (pigmies or otherwise) falls into the realm of cryptozoology,[26] a pseudoscience which basically covers a quest or search for animals whose existence has not been proven. It covers areas such as the hunt for Bigfoot and the Yeti and other creatures whose existence is anecdotal and reports of sightings lack solid evidence. The person who is often attributed to having expanded the usage of the term cryptozoology, Bernard Heuvelmans, felt that although much of the anecdotal evidence and stories originating in folklore may not have had a solid scientific base, he felt that there was an element of truth in many sightings and that this could form the basis for moving the study forward with a more scientific approach. The animals studied by the cryptozoologists are known as cryptids.[27]

There is no shortage of these cryptids in the islands of the north-west and north of Scotland. Sea monsters in particular have been sighted on numerous occasions off the coast of Lewis. One notable sighting took place in 1882 when the crew of a German ship, 9 miles (15km) off the Butt of Lewis, reported seeing a giant sea serpent approximately 131ft (40m) in length with a series of bumps along its back. The Butt of Lewis is only 50 miles (80km) from the Flannan Isles, and it was at this location the *Archtor* was to pass eighteen years later after passing the darkened lighthouse on Eilean Mor. There have been other sightings of sea serpents in the seas off Lewis, notably on the southern side of the island.[28] A more recent sighting took place in the summer of 1959 off Barra.[29]

The Beast of Stronsay[30] was also said to inhabit the waters in this region, although it was sighted nearer to Orkney. The beast was first sighted at Stronsay, Orkney, on 25 September 1808, lying on rocks on the south-east of the island on Rothiesholm Head. On that day, a local man, John Peace was fishing off the coast when he noticed what appeared to be seagulls feasting on an animal's carcass. Intrigued by what he was observing, Peace turned his boat to go and investigate. When he got there he found a very strange-looking creature, unlike anything he had seen before. The scene was also observed by another Stronsay inhabitant, George Sherar. The creature that was lying decomposing on the rocks was of a large serpent type, with a long eel-like neck and three pairs of legs. Sherar was unable to get too close, as the carcass was inaccessible. Ten days later a gale blew the remains above the high-water mark and a closer examination was possible. Sherar made measurements and studied the carcass, which he described as serpentine. It was exactly 55ft long with a neck that was 10ft 3in long. The skin was grey and rough, although if the skin was rubbed from the head down the back 'it was smooth as velvet to the touch'. Sherar described the head of the beast as similar to that of a sheep and the eyes were bigger than a seal's. There were six limbs which extended from the body along with a bristly mane of long, wiry hair which grew down to the tail. The bristles were silver coloured and said to 'glow eerily in the dark'. The local newspaper *the Orcadian*, reported the find: 'Its flesh was described as being like "coarse, ill-coloured beef, entirely covered with fat and tallow and without the least resemblance of or affinity to fish. The skin which was grey coloured and had an elastic texture was said to be about two inches thick in parts."'

By the end of that September, news of the Stronsay beast had spread far and wide. However, the carcass had rotted away so much that the four men who had seen the beast went to Kirkwall to swear to a magistrate that their account was truthful.

The Stronsay beast was discussed at a meeting of the Natural History Society in Edinburgh in November 1808. The Beast was given the Latin name *Halsydrus Pontoppidani* which meant 'Pontoppidan's Water Snake of the Sea'. The name was in honour of the Norwegian Bishop of Bergen, Erik Pontoppidan, who collected reports of sea monsters.

A more sceptical view was taken by the naturalist Sir Everard Home. He viewed what was left of the carcass and concluded after examining the vertebrae that it was the remains of a basking shark, a creature which was commonly found in Scottish waters. Apparently the remains of a basking shark as it decomposes were similar to the description given by the four witnesses in Kirkwall. As a basking shark decomposes, the jaws (which are only held on by a small piece of flesh) drop off, leaving what looks like a long neck and a small head. After this, as only the upper half of the shark's tail fin contains the spine, the lower half rots away and leaves what looks like a long serpentine spine. When the dorsal fin begins to decompose, this can give the appearance of a hair-like mane. The six leg-like appendages noted by Sherar and the others can be explained away by the shark's lower fins rotting away.

Despite these arguments against the Stronsay beast being genuine, it has been said that the longest basking shark ever measured was only 40ft; the 55ft measurement of the Stronsay Beast is considerably larger. So, is it possible there are other serpentine creatures of a similar size to the Stronsay beast in the waters of northern Scotland?

In terms of the supernatural, a rather odd report came from a seaman on a passing ship[31] who stated that he had seen three men in a rowing boat passing by his ship close to the Flannan Isles. This sighting (which was deemed to have a ghostly appearance) was around the time of the incident at Eilean Mor. The seaman on the ship called out to the three men in the rowing boat but they ignored his calls and carried on rowing. Despite the veracity of this account, the three men were unlikely to have been the missing lightkeepers. They had no boat on Eilean Mor, for the simple reason that it was virtually impossible to keep a boat there and launch it, as any boat kept close to the waterline would have either been destroyed in bad weather or swept away.

Finally, after having considered the folklore of the Outer Hebrides and the various possibilities of the disappearance of the three men being somehow connected to a supernatural event, there is one last possibility of the Flannan Islands visiting a curse upon the lighthousemen and anything connected with the lighthouse on Eilean Mor.

There were, of course, plenty of lightkeepers who followed Ducat, Marshall and Macarthur onto the light station on Eilean Mor; however, there are some aspects worth considering. It could be said that a series of incidents connected to a person or a place could be ascribed to just bad luck or unfortunate coincidence. However, there was a series of unfortunate occurrences connected with the lighthouse, right from the time it was being constructed.

First, there was a death during the construction phase of the light station when, at the end of the third season of work, the Clerk of Works, Mr Deas, suddenly passed away. Just over a year later, the three lightkeepers disappeared. Next, on that night of 15–16 December 1900, when the SS *Archtor* passed the Flannans and saw the light was not operational, she hit the Carphie Rock within forty-eight hours of passing and, severely damaged, limped to the port of Leith. Then in an episode reminiscent of the missing lightkeepers, the *Archtor* herself disappeared without trace on or about 4 January 1912. She left Norfolk, Virginia, on 2 January 1912 for Rotterdam with a cargo of phosphate rock. The *Archtor* was seen passing Cape Henry on the following day, 3 January 1912. After that last sighting she was never seen or heard from again. She was widely believed to have sunk with all hands in very bad weather at some point in the North Atlantic, shortly after passing Cape Henry, but as with the missing lightkeepers of Eilean Mor, there was no proof of what actually happened to her.

Of the men who replaced the missing lightkeepers, for one of them it was to be his final posting (*see* Chapter 5). John McLachlan arrived as one of the replacements on 29 January 1901. On 20 August 1904 he fell from the Eilean Mor light tower and was killed.

William Ross, who was one of the resident lightkeepers on Eilean Mor, should have been present at the station on Saturday 15 December 1900. He was ill in Breasclete and was being covered by Donald Macarthur on that date. At the time he was an ALK and was transferred to the Sound of Mull from the Flannan Isles on 1 February 1901. He was promoted to PLK on 6 September 1901 before being transferred to Eilean Glas Lighthouse from the Sound of Mull. On 15 April 1902, one year and four months to the day after the disappearances, Ross dropped dead in the lightroom at Eilean Glas. As has been mentioned, it could be said to be unfortunate coincidences that two lightkeepers had connections to James Ducat, Thomas Marshall and Donald Macarthur, and it could be said that it is unfortunate coincidence that the deaths of these two men both took place in or on a light tower, one of them being the Eilean Mor Lighthouse itself.

Notes

1. This book can be downloaded and read in its entirety from www.archive.org.
2. *Travels to Terra Incognita* by Martin Rackwitz, Waxmann Verlag GmbH, 2007. An excellent and very readable book, which is probably better for those who do not wish to plough through the older English in Martin Martin's book.
3. The correct name of the vessel was *Mary Celeste*, it is often called the *Marie Celeste* in error – this was the name given to the vessel by Arthur Conan Doyle in his fictional account.
4. *Baffling Mysteries: A Collection of Weird Problems and Unsolved Riddles* by Cary Miller, 1976, pp. 19–27.
5. Memo from the superintendent to Robert Muirhead regarding the necessity for transferring J. Moore, assistant keeper, Flannan Isles, 15 January 1901.
6. Extract of text from copy of telegram from Captain Harvey, Scottish National Archive file no. NLC3/1/1.
7. *The Flying Saucer Vision* by John Michell, Abacus, 1974, pp. 113–17.
8. Ibid.
9. The film, which was remade in 2006, was based on the novel *Ritual* by David Pinner.
10. *The Flying Saucer Vision* by John Michell, Abacus, 1974, pp. 113–17.
11. Ibid.
12. en.wikipedia.org/wiki/Hebridean_Mythology_and_folklore.
13. *The Flying Saucer Vision*, John Michell, Abacus, 1974, pp. 113–17.
14. *Vanishings* by Michael Harrison, New English Library, 1981, pp. 119–23
15. Ibid.
16. For instance, see 'The Flannan Isles', by Mark Fraser, in *Haunted Scotland*, issue 7, 1997.
17. *Description of the Western Isles of Scotland* by Donald Monro, 1774.
18. *Description of Lewis* by Captain John Dymes, 1630.
19. *A Description of the Western Isles of Scotland* by Martin Martin, 1703.
20. The bulk of the information in this section comes from an article by W.C. MacKenzie.
21. Ibid.
22. Ibid.
23. Ibid.
24. Ibid.
25. Ibid.
26. A term coined by Scottish adventurer and explorer Ivan T. Sanderson and expanded in usage by Bernard Heuvelmans, a Belgian-French

zoologist. The term is from *kryptos* meaning 'hidden' and *zoology* meaning 'study of animals'.
27 en.wikipedia.org/wiki/Cryptid.
28 en.wikipedia.org/Hebridean_mythology_and_folklore.
29 *Ring of Bright Water* by Gavin Maxwell.
30 Account from Orkneyjar, www.orkneyjar.com/folklore/seabeasts.htm. The Stronsay beast details given by kind permission of Sigurd Towrie.
31 The exact source and further details are unclear.

Conclusions

It is well over 100 years since the disaster, and the Flannan Isles, along with the lighthouse station, are little changed from that day in December 1900. After it was automated in 1971, there was no longer any need for a human presence there. The main change is the building of a helicopter landing pad not far from the stone chapel, giving an almost surreal aspect. There are, however, still visitors who arrive by launch on day trips from the west coast of Lewis, a service run by Seatrek in the summer. The run is very popular with people interested in the islands and particularly for birdwatchers, who have plenty to see with the colonies of puffins, gannets and other seabirds.

The Stones at Callanish also draw plenty of interest. There is also much in the area to explore on a holiday and visitors can see the former Flannan Isles shore station in Breasclete, which was taken over by the local council and converted into flats.

The NLB headquarters at 84 George Street in Edinburgh are in the same Georgian building they have always occupied, and around the Scottish coast the lighthouses remain; most are still working but others have been sold off. At virtually every station the lightkeeper's cottages have been sold into private ownership, although the NLB has retained the towers. Passing ships were and still are charged so much per ton of cargo carried, length of vessel etc.; this money being paid into the

General Lighthouse Fund. The system is more complicated than this now, as all kinds of scales and charges are worked out and agreed with shipowners and there are various kinds of exceptions and exemptions. It is not perhaps generally realised that, at least as far as the UK and Ireland are concerned, the three lighthouse authorities are entirely self-funding, receiving no government money at all.

Anna (Annabella) Ducat who was eight years old[1] at the time of her father's disappearance, gave an interview to *The Times* in 1990[2] when she was ninety-eight years old and living in Edinburgh. The article gave brief details of the circumstances of the disappearances. Anna Ducat had stated that her father had been reluctant to take the Flannan Isles posting when it was offered to him by Robert Muirhead. He had said that it was too dangerous and that he had a wife and four children depending on him, but took the position when pressed by Muirhead, who had faith in his abilities as a good lightkeeper. She mentioned that six months previous to the disappearance, her father had been fined 5s for damage to landing tackle at the west landing; as such, her view was that her father had gone down to check the equipment with Marshall on Saturday 15 December when the winds had moderated[3] and that a freak wave had swept them away. There is no mention of the fine in the archive records at the Scottish National Archives. This of course is not to say that he was not fined. Not all the records are available in the archives but there is the detail concerning the near accident to the crane caused by Thomas Marshall's carelessness and as both men were involved in this, it is more likely that this was the driving factor behind the decision of the men to approach the west landing.

The mystery of what happened to James Ducat, Thomas Marshall and Donald Macarthur generates as much speculation now as it probably did at the time, with the various theories mulled over time and again. The weight of evidence supports the giant wave theory. However, virtually every former lightkeeper interviewed for this book has said that under normal circumstances, in bad weather, no one would have ventured outside, particularly in conditions as treacherous as they were that Saturday afternoon. Another point to bear in mind is that, assuming they took an hour for lunch at 1 p.m. that day, there was less than an hour and a half of full daylight left when they ventured outside.

A normal day saw the majority of work undertaken in the mornings, with rest being taken in the afternoons before night duty. Something took the pair (or all three) down to the west landing on that last day, in the afternoon, in weather that generally would have precluded anyone from leaving the safety and security of the lighthouse.

There would have been plenty of tasks for them to do indoors during bad weather, such as cleaning the lens and doing the brasswork – two of many tasks that always had to be carried out – yet they went outside. Did their fear of being fined for loss of equipment override their caution? In 1900, 5s would have been considered a tidy sum, therefore had they been fined this amount some time previously, as seems likely, then this could have accounted for what may have seemed extreme foolhardiness.

It is quite likely that the three men would have been anxious to avoid a repetition of damage or loss involving them in a fine, especially at Christmas time. There can have been no other practical reason for them descending to the west landing, other than to check that the ropes and tackle were secured and thus avoid the possibility of another fine. One has to ask what was so pressing. What made them think that the ropes and tackle were not secure? Are we to assume that a man with twenty-two years of lightkeeping behind him, and experience of the dangers of the sea, literally threw all caution to the wind and risked his life and that of his two colleagues for the sake of avoiding a fine? In view of the fact that there was just over an hour of full daylight left and that they would have been facing massive waves on their descent down to the west landing it must be said that this theory is as implausible as any of the others.

Despite the possibility of Walter Aldebert's theory, there is also another scenario which would explain the visit of Muirhead and his wife on 7 December 1900 (an odd time of year for the superintendent and his wife to visit considering the weather and difficulties of landing on Eilean Mor in winter). The strong possibility is that there was growing tension over the months at Breasclete and on the rock between the volatile Donald Macarthur (who was known to be argumentative and hot headed) and James Ducat which Muirhead was trying to resolve on his visit, as the Flannans was his pet project. After his visit, tensions erupted again on the 15 December when Ducat asked Macarthur to accompany him to go down to secure the crane and box of ropes on the West landing. There was a violent disagreement about this between Macarthur and Ducat, so Ducat went with Marshall instead, despite the weather, the size of the waves and the dwindling light. Macarthur was fuming about the exchange and went after them in a rage without his 'wearing coat'. Despite being a short man, Macarthur's temper had got the better of him. he had spent nearly the whole previous two months on the station covering for Ross, and his rage boiled over. Ducat's request on top of his other work as duty cook was the final straw. He caught up with them just before the start of the steps by the steep cliff, and a fight broke out. Marshall tried to intervene and his momentum carried all three of them over the cliff and on to the rocks and boiling sea 110ft below.

Notes
1. The *Times* article stated she was eight years old. Correspondence regarding pensions and annuities for James Ducat by the NLB stated she was nine years old. Interview, 'Boxing Day on Flannan Rock' with Anna Ducat by Joan Simpson, *The Times*, 26 December 1990.
2. Interview 'Boxing Day on Flannan Rock', with Anna Ducat by Joan Simpson, *The Times*, 26 December 1990.
3. The Met Office records for that day show that the winds were actually increasing in strength throughout the day – see Appendix III.

Appendix I

'Flannan Isle'

Though three men dwell on Flannan Isle
To keep the lamp alight,
As we steer'd under the lee, we caught
No glimmer through the night!

A passing ship at dawn had brought
The news; and quickly we set sail,
To find out what strange thing might ail
The keepers of the deep-sea light.

The winter day broke blue and bright,
With glancing sun and glancing spray,
As o'er the swell our boat made way,
As gallant as a gull in flight.

But, as we near'd the lonely Isle;
And look'd up at the naked height;
And saw the lighthouse towering white,
With blinded lantern, that all night
Had never shot a spark
Of comfort through the dark,
So ghastly in the cold sunlight
It seem'd, that we were struck the while
With wonder all too dread for words.

And, as into the tiny creek
We stole beneath the hanging crag,
We saw three queer, black, ugly birds –
Too big, by far, in my belief,
For guillemot or shag –
Like seamen sitting bold upright
Upon a half-tide reef:
But, as we near'd, they plunged from sight,
Without a sound, or spurt of white.

And still too mazed to speak,
We landed; and made fast the boat;
And climb'd the track in single file,
Each wishing he was safe afloat,
On any sea, however far,
So it be far from Flannan Isle:
And still we seem'd to climb, and climb,
As though we'd lost all count of time,
And so must climb for evermore.
Yet, all too soon, we reached the door –
The black, sun-blister'd lighthouse door,
That gaped for us ajar.

As, on the threshold, for a spell,
We paused, we seem'd to breathe the smell
Of limewash and of tar,
Familiar as our daily breath,
As though 'twere some strange scent of death:
And so, yet wondering, side by side,
We stood a moment, still tongue-tied:
And each with black foreboding eyed
The door, ere we should fling it wide,
To leave the sunlight for the gloom:
Till, plucking courage up, at last,
Hard on each other's heels we pass'd
Into the living-room.

Yet, as we crowded through the door,
We only saw a table, spread
For dinner, meat and cheese and bread;
But all untouch'd; and no one there:
As though, when they sat down to eat,
Ere they could even taste,
Alarm had come; and they in haste
Had risen and left the bread and meat:
For on the table-head a chair
Lay tumbled on the floor.
We listen'd; but we only heard
The feeble cheeping of a bird
That starved upon its perch:
And, listening still, without a word,
We set about our hopeless search.

We hunted high, we hunted low,
And soon ransack'd the empty house;
Then o'er the Island, to and fro,
We ranged, to listen and to look
In every cranny, cleft or nook
That might have hid a bird or mouse:
But, though we searched from shore to shore,
We found no sign in any place:
And soon again stood face to face
Before the gaping door:
And stole into the room once more
As frighten'd children steal.

Aye: though we hunted high and low,
And hunted everywhere,
Of the three men's fate we found no trace
Of any kind in any place,
But a door ajar, and an untouch'd meal,
And an overtoppled chair.

And, as we listen'd in the gloom
Of that forsaken living-room -
O chill clutch on our breath -
We thought how ill-chance came to all
Who kept the Flannan Light:
And how the rock had been the death
Of many a likely lad:
How six had come to a sudden end
And three had gone stark mad:
And one whom we'd all known as friend
Had leapt from the lantern one still night,
And fallen dead by the lighthouse wall:
And long we thought
On the three we sought,
And of what might yet befall.

Like curs a glance has brought to heel,
We listen'd, flinching there:
And look'd, and look'd, on the untouch'd meal
And the overtoppled chair.

We seem'd to stand for an endless while,
Though still no word was said,
Three men alive on Flannan Isle,
Who thought on three men dead.

Wilfrid Wilson Gibson
© *Trustees of the Gibson Estate*

Appendix II

ABSTRACT OF SIGNALMAN'S RETURNS (RODERICK MacKENZIE) FOR FLANNAN ISLES LIGHTHOUSE

	Tower		Light	
(Days)	Seen	Not Seen	Seen	Not Seen
1900				
February	16	12	–	–
March	17	14	17	8
April	13	17	19	10
May	14	17	17	14
June	15	15	22	8
July	17	14	22	9
August	17	14	25	6
September	5	25	22	8
October	12	19	26	4
November	7	23	27	2
December	7	24	13	17
1901				
January	6	25	22	9

Note – In 1900 the signalman did not mark the nights on which the light was seen or not seen until instructed to do so in the beginning of March, when it was observed from his February return that he had not been doing so.

Appendix III

WEATHER DETAILS

Basic summary of weather (excluding barometer and temperature readings) in Flannan Isles/Lewis area from 12 December 1900 to arrival of *Hesperus* at Eilean Mor on 26 December 1900:

Wednesday 12 December

Rainfall in the afternoon and early evening. Strong westerly winds at 8 a.m., which had shifted to south-westerly by 6 p.m.

Thursday 13 December

Rainfall in the morning. Strong south-westerly gale force winds in the morning, veering to westwards by the afternoon. Charts showing a disturbed sea state around the Flannans and whole north-west sea area in general.

Friday 14 December

Rainfall in the morning and throughout the day. Strong south-westerly gale-force winds, with charts showing a very disturbed sea state around the Flannans and Hebrides

Saturday 15 December (date of disappearance)

The weather for the date of the disappearance was west-south-west force 7 at 8 a.m., (note: at 9 a.m. the Flannans slate showed westerly winds, occasionally blustery showers – from Joseph Moore's report), south-west force 8^1 at 2 p.m. and north-west force 9^2 at 6 p.m. As the wind and waves grew in strength and moved around from the south-west after 2 p.m., they would have been directed, more or less, straight onto the west landing.

Sunday 16 December

Strong south-westerly gale force winds, with the charts for that day showing a disturbed sea in the area.

Monday 17 December

A violent storm coming from the South West centered directly over the Flannan Isles with winds and waves just below hurricane force. Waves of 75ft would have been likely due to the long build-up area (fetch) approaching the Flannans.

Tuesday 18 December

Previous day's violent storm passed to leave a fine day, light breeze.

Wednesday 19 December

The day started fine with a light to moderate southerly wind later moving to westerly. Light rainfall later in the day which turned heavy.

Thursday 20 December (date of severe gales over Britain with Scotland hit hardest)

Weather generally described overall as disturbed and rough in summing up. Some accounts have stated storm conditions, but met office records state severe gales from south-westerly turning to north-westerly. Light rainfall.

Friday 21 December

Disturbed sea state, squally rain, westerly gales moderating later.

Saturday 22 December

Generally fine day, although there was light rainfall in later morning and afternoon. Moderate to light winds.

Sunday 23 December

Cloudy and dull with rainfall. A light south-easterly wind which veered around to the south-west through the course of the day.

Monday 24 December

Started as a fine day but heavy rainfall later. A strong south-westerly wind which had increased to gale force by 6 p.m.

Tuesday 25 December

Cloudy and unsettled with rain. Strong to gale force south-westerly winds at 8 a.m., which moderated as day went on and winds veered to westward.

Wednesday 26 December (arrival of *Hesperus*)

The weather was fine in the morning with some showers which increased to heavier rain later in the day. A moderate to strong wind was blowing from the south-west. Charts show a disturbed sea state to the north of the Flannan Isles.

Above details courtesy of the Met Office National Meteorological Archive, Exeter.

Notes
1. Force 8 = Moderately high waves with breaking crests forming spindrift. Well-marked streaks of foam are blown along wind direction. Considerable airborne spray. Waves up to 25ft.
2. Force 9 = High waves whose crests sometimes roll over. Dense foam is blown along wind direction. Large amounts of airborne spray may begin to reduce visibility. Waves up to 32ft.

Appendix IV

RECOLLECTIONS OF THE EILEAN MOR LIGHTHOUSE BY NORRIE MUIR PLK

I was appointed as an assistant keeper on the 1 May 1963 and my pay would be £544 per annum. My victualing allowance would be 5/3p per day. On 2 May 1963 I had to go out to the lighthouse for two calendar months – after my two months on the rock I would get one month ashore. I was taken out to the light by the MV *Pole Star*. The Flannan Islands are 20 miles off the coast of Lewis and it was a two and a half hour trip in bad weather which was not very nice. When we got to the light, the ship would put the launch in the water to take us to the landing, we could not go alongside so the keepers on the rock would put a rope down to pull the keeper going on the rock up on to the landing along with the provisions to do us for our first month on the rock. When the keepers that were leaving went ashore that was the last we would see another ship or fresh food for a month. When I got up to the light I got the fright of my life, it was just the same as it was in 1900, there was no modern amenities at all. The kitchen had the same coal range, the light in the kitchen was a paraffin lamp that you had to pump air into it to keep it going as it had a mantel, the table was in the same place by the window as it was in 1900, the small bedrooms were just the same as they had two bunks in each of the three bedrooms all adjoining the kitchen. The only thing that we did have which the old keepers did not have was a gas cooker and a paraffin refrigerator and if you did not get the flame right, it would not work.

We did have two small generators to charge the batteries but they were for our VHF communications. We had to phone the Butt of Lewis every day but you could not talk for very long or the battery would run down as they were very old and would not hold the charge. We did have an old radio with an old accumulator, there was no TV. The Flannans was known as the 'OK Rock' as that was all we had time to send (as a message)! The principal's word was law, you did what you were told. He made the rules right down to what we ate. He had a menu on the wall and it was the same menu every week. Breakfast Monday to Friday would be porridge, you had three slices of bread a day – if you had two slices of bread for breakfast you only got one slice for tea. The one thing I have never forgotten was we would get fish on a Friday: Week one – OK, Week two – not too bad, Week three – you could eat it, Week four – forget it, I'll just have beans and chips! That would be the same in 1900 as you would not get any more food until the next relief. I thought that when I went ashore I would get some flour to make some bread. The bread went off after week two so I had to soak it in water and dry it off on the range and by week four I had to cut the fungus off. Well when I went back onto the rock the principal went mad and he said that he did not tell me to get any flour so I had to pay for it myself. That was the way it was, you only did as you were told as it would have been in 1900.

This is very important, the Northern Lighthouse Board did not know what was going on at the light as long as the station was clean and the light was in good order, they were happy. We would have a visit from the district superintendent, he and two artificers would arrive to maintain all the machinery. The superintendent would ask the principal if things were alright, 'Oh Yes' he would say as he and the keepers would not say a word as they were too frightened to tell the super and that is the way it was. The office were [sic] God and it would be the same in 1900 if not more so.

Now for the landings, we had two landings, one at the east and one at the west. The east landing was the best one as it had some shelter and we did most of the reliefs at that landing. It had a steel crane with an engine, but if the weather was bad we had to use the west landing and it was the very same as it was in 1900, the only difference was we had a steel crane but it had handles on it. The keepers in 1900 would have had a wooden derrick. The crane was 70ft above the west landing and the sea in bad weather would come around the corner of the west landing and solid water would crash into the landing. There would be up to 100ft of solid water and the power of the sea was frightening as it would take all in its path. I was talking to an old man in Lewis and he said that the keepers on the Flannans had lost the wooden derrick as the sea at the west landing had washed it away if this is true.* My theory is that the Lighthouse Board would replace the wooden derrick and the keepers would be told to put more ropes on the derrick in bad weather. Now in the light if the keepers were having a meal or sitting at the table, they would be looking out of the window, they could not see the west landing but there was a blow hole and if the sea was rough, the sea would come up through the blow hole up to 100ft in the air [and] that would tell the keepers that the west landing was getting a hammering by the sea. I was once told by an old seaman that in a rough sea, every seventh wave was a big one. If it was daylight I would think that all the keepers would go down to the landing to see what was going on. Keepers don't like to miss things, I am the same today. If the keepers went down to put more rope on the derrick and if a big wave came around the corner they would have had no chance with that power and that weight of water,

---

* One of the cranes on the west landing was washed away in 1899 – see Chapter 6.

they would have no hope of getting out of that, they would be just swept away. That is my theory but I can't say I am right. I had five years on the Flannans and I did thirty-two and a half years in the lighthouse service, it was a grand job.

Norrie Muir was an ALK on the Flannan Isles and this account is published with his kind permission.

Appendix V

EILEAN MOR LIGHTHOUSE PRAYER

After a Storm or Signal Escape from Danger

Thou, in whom alone we live, and move, and have our being, we desire to offer unto thee humble and hearty thanks for that signal instance of thy protecting care which we have been permitted to experience. When human aid availeth not, thou art mighty to save. O may we render unto thee alone the glory and the praise.

May the danger to which we have been exposed, stir us up to greater earnestness in our preparation for eternity. May the deliverance which hath been vouchsafed to us – while it fills our heart with gratitude, and our tongue with praise – establish the more our trust in the living God; and make us the more willing to meet danger again, when the discharge of our duty demands it.

Repeated from memory (from the Prayer Book held at Eilean Mor Lighthouse) by kind courtesy of Norrie Muir who was an Assistant Lightkeeper (ALK) on the Flannan Isles.

SOURCES AND FURTHER READING

Books

Bathurst, Bella, *The Lighthouse Stevensons*, Harper Perennial, 1999
Curran, Dr Bob, *World's Creepiest Places*, New Page, 2011
Elliott, Angela J., *Some Strange Scent of Death*, Whittles, 2005
Gaddis, Vincent, *Invisible Horizons*, Ace Star Books, reprinted by arrangement with Chilton Books USA, 1965
Harrison, Michael, *Vanishings*, New English Library, 1981
Hill, Peter, *Stargazing: Memoirs of a Young Lighthouse Keeper*, Canongate Books, 2003
Mair, Craig, *A Star for Seamen*, John Murray, 1978
Martin Martin, *A Description of the Western Isles of Scotland*, 1703
Miller, Carey, *Baffling Mysteries*, Piccolo, 1976
Mitchell, John, *The Flying Saucer Vision*, Abacus, 1974
Nicholson, Christopher, *Rock Lighthouses of Britain*, Whittles Publishing, 1995
Parker, Tony, *Lighthouse*, Eland, 1986
Rackwitz, Martin, *Travels to Terra Incognita: The Scottish Highlands and Hebrides in Early Modern Travellers' Accounts c.1600–1800*, Waxman Verlag GmbH, 2007
Ryan, Sheila, *Untold Stories: Beachy Head*, SB Publishing, 2010

Magazines and Newspapers

(Aberdeen) Press and Journal
Haunted Scotland
NLB house magazine
Oban Times
Oban Express
Scotsman
Scottish Islands Explorer Magazine
The Times

Websites

www.metoffice.gov.uk/learning/library
www.nas.gov.uk
www.nls.uk
www.orkneyjar.com/folklore/seabeasts.htm

INDEX

Agulhas Current 140
Aldebert, Walter Robert 142–4, 200
Andrews, Dr Charles W. 187
Angus, Iain 145
Anstruther 67, 151
Arbroath 55
Archtor 11–12, 65–70, 74, 87, 190, 193
Arthur M. Anderson 137–9

Badenstein 134
Beag, Niall 145
Beddoe, Dr John 188
Beggs, William (PLK) 9, 93–5
Bell Rock 44–5, 65–6, 94
Blaeu, Willem 181
'Blessing Chapel' 26, 108
Boat, William (NLB Acct.) 98, 104
Bond Helicopters 44
Breasclete (Breascleit) 18, 25, 28, 32, 56–7, 59, 89, 94, 106–7, 112, 114–15, 147–8, 163, 174–5, 193, 197, 200
Brown, David 99–101, 117
Bryant, Martin 159
Buchanan, George 108, 180, 182
Buckey Jr, Dr. Jay C. 149, 172
Buddon Ness, 22
Butt of Lewis 12, 25, 39–40, 105, 179, 182, 185, 190, 212

Callanish Stones 15–16
Cape Wrath 32
Caribe 133
Carloway 28, 108, 178
Carphie Rock 14, 66–8, 87, 193
Chesapeake 65
Chicken Rock 50–1, 150
Clark, Rita Pearl 160–2
Collin, David 151–4, 172
Collins, William 181
Copinsay 32

Delting Disaster 1900 122
Derbyshire 140–6
Dick Peddie, Coventry, NLB Secretary 99–101
Dickson, Robert 154
Don Carlos 135
Douglas Head 171
Douglas, N.J., Crown Agent 157
Douglass, James (Trinity House) 157
'Draupner Wave' 141
Dubh'Artach 50
Ducat, Annabella (Child) 97–8, 198
Ducat, Arthur (Child) 97
Ducat, James (PLK) 39, 42, 54–64, 71–2, 74–8, 80, 82, 84–5, 90, 93, 95, 97, 107, 112, 116, 119, 121–7, 132, 143–4, 146, 163–4, 169, 175, 177, 192–3, 198, 200
Ducat, Louisa (Child) 97–8
Ducat, Mrs Mary (Wife) 98
Ducat, Robert (Child) 97–8
Dun Carloway 178
Dusseldorf Express 135
Dymes, Captain John 180–2, 194

Eagle Island Lighthouses 128, 130–2
east landing 57, 73–4, 81, 119, 165, 213
Eddystone 157
Edmund Fitzgerald 136–9, 142, 146

Eilean Glas 193
Elkhart Truth 84
Ergot 165–9, 172
Erlangen 134
Ernst, Jorg 133
Evelyn 135

Fallon, Ernest 85
Faulkner, Prof. Douglas 140
Foghorn 30, 42–3, 53

Gaddis, Vincent Hayes 84, 218
Gallan Head 13, 25, 69, 109
George Lawson (Contractor) 114
George Street, 84 (NLB HQ) 29, 37, 42–3, 50, 55, 62, 79, 96, 104, 124, 126, 143–4, 151, 197
Granton 32, 89
Greenheart Logs 123
Griffiths, Tom 156–7

Haar 21, 54
Halsydrus Pontoppidani 191
Harvie/Harvey, Captain James 70–4, 80–1, 88–9, 104, 106–7, 176, 194
Hesperus, NLB Tender 57, 70–1, 73, 88–93, 104–7, 111–13, 172–3, 175–6, 179, 207, 210
Heuvelmans, Bernard 189, 195
Hochelaga 137
Holman, Captain 11–14, 65–70, 74, 87
Howells, Tom 156–7
Hyskeir 95, 127

Index

Inchkeith 55, 67–8, 142
Irish Lights 22, 49
Isle of Man 22, 49, 51, 116, 149–50
Isle of May 22, 151
Isle of Pigmies 181–2

Jack, Donald (NLB Storeman) 72, 79, 89–90

King George 134
Kinnaird Head 22

Lamont, A. 73, 76, 81, 91
Lang, Effie (witch) 151
Langness 55
LASH 132, 146
Launceston, Tasmania 161
Leith 11-12, 65, 67–8, 87, 193
Loch Roag 19, 28, 70–1, 105–8, 115
Lossiemouth 45, 53, 103
Luchruban 181, 186–9

Macarthur, Donald 42, 54, 56–61, 63–4, 72, 76, 78, 80, 82, 84, 90, 95–6, 102, 116–17, 119–21, 123, 126–7, 132, 143–4, 163–5, 169, 175, 177, 192–3, 198, 200
MacBain, Dr. Alexander 180
Mackenzie, C.G 182
Mackenzie, Dr. 182–5
Mackenzie, Robert (Lookout) 13–14, 69–70, 76–7, 113–14
Mackenzie, W.C. 179, 181–2, 185–9, 194

MacLeod, Donald John (father) 147–8
MacLeod, Donald John (son) 147–8, 164
Marshall, John 99–102, 117
Marshall, Thomas 42, 54, 56, 58–64, 71–2, 75, 78, 80, 82–7, 90, 95, 97–101, 103, 107, 115–16, 119, 121–7, 132, 143–4, 163, 165, 169, 175, 177, 192–3, 198, 200
Martin, Martin 109, 173, 176, 180–1, 187, 194, 218
McEachearn, Angus 92–5
McLachlan, John 93–5, 193
McSorley, Captain 138–9
Milne, John N. 72, 79, 89, 90
Monach 25
Monro, Dean 180, 182–3, 185, 187
Moore, Joseph 56, 70–3, 75–7, 80, 82–3, 85–6, 88, 90–4, 116, 121, 127, 164, 168, 174–6, 179, 194, 208
Mornington, Victoria 161–2
Muir Cul 145
Muirhead, Robert 69, 71–2, 79–80, 83, 85–95, 112–14, 116–17, 119, 121–2, 127, 144–6, 168–71, 175, 179, 194, 198, 200
Munchen 132–5, 142, 146
Murdoch, James (NLB Sec.) 60, 71, 89–90, 96, 99, 104, 111–12, 124–6, 146, 170, 176

Nilssen, Prof. Sven 188
Norddeich Radio 134
North Carr Light Vessel 65, 66

Oban 32, 42, 70, 72, 87, 106, 112
Osborne, Frederick 158–9

Parker, Tony 127, 146, 217
Peace, John 190
Pentland Skerries 32
Peterhead 44, 53
Pharos, NLB Tender 115
Phillips, John 155
Pied Piper of Hamelin 167–8, 172
Pladda 32
Poland, George 153
Pole Star, NLB Tender 27–8, 50, 125, 146, 148, 211

RAF Leuchars 44–5
Rathlin Island 47
Rattray Head 53
Report (J. Moore) 80–2
Report (R. Muirhead) 72–9
Rhinns of Islay 55, 142
Ross, David 93–5
Ross, Jack 144, 146
Ross, William 39, 56–7, 59, 72, 95–6, 117, 193
Rubh'Re 33

Saint Frangus 178, 186
Salem Witch Trials 167, 172
Sanda 32, 44, 48

Scotsman 54, 64, 104, 109, 111–12, 117, 145, 218
Scurdieness 55
Sealand Consumer 135
Skerryvore 43, 51, 56
Smalls Lighthouse 155–7, 163, 172
Smit Rotterdam 134
Smith, Thomas 231
Sound of Mull 193
South Fair Isle Lighthouse 52
St. Flannan 17, 19
St. Simons Island 157–8, 172
Stephens, John 158
Stevenson, Alan 24
Stevenson, Charles 25
Stevenson, David A. 18, 24–9, 36, 52, 54, 94, 105, 114–15, 117
Stevenson, Jean 23
Stevenson, Robert 23
Stevenson, Robert Louis 23–4
Stevenson, Thomas 25
Storm Kelpies 178
Stornoway 72, 90, 104, 107, 111, 182
Stroma 32, 36
Stromness 18, 27–8, 32, 50, 148
Stronsay Beast 9, 191–2, 195
Sule Skerry 28, 32, 50, 103, 124–5, 142
Svendson, Carl 158–9

'Three Sisters' 136, 138, 141
Times, The 127, 146, 198, 200, 218

Titan 133–4
Tiumpan Head 72, 89–90
Tory Island Lighthouse 130
Tregenza, Robert-Patrick (Bob) 160–2
Trinity House 22, 38, 49, 155, 157, 170
Tsunami 141–2

West landing 26, 59–61, 63–4, 70, 74–5, 81, 86, 91, 115, 119–24, 126–7, 132, 142–5, 165, 169, 171, 198–200, 208, 213
Whiteside, Henry 155
Wicker Man 177

Yates, Herbert James 160–2

If you enjoyed this book, you may also be interested in…

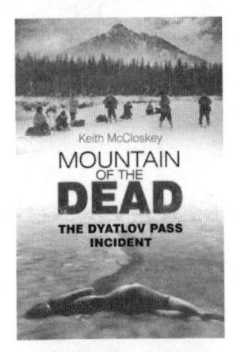

Mountain of the Dead
KEITH MCCLOSKEY

January 1959. Nine experienced young skiers lose their way and ended up on a mountain slope known as the Mountain of the Dead. On the night of 1 February, something or someone caused the skiers to flee their tent in such terror that they used knives to slash their way out …

978 0 7524 9148 6

The Poltergeist Prince of London
JAMES CLARK & SHIRLEY HITCHINGS

One of the most mysterious hauntings in British history. The spirit, who quickly became known as 'Donald', began to communicate by learning to write. Soon, the spirit had begun to make simply incredible claims about his identity, Here, for the first time, is the full story, told by the woman at the heart of it all.

978 0 7524 9803 4

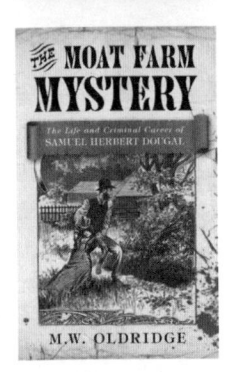

The Moat Farm Mystery
M.W. OLDRIDGE

Samuel Herbert Dougal was intelligent, talented, and the recipient of a military medal. But he was also a career criminal whose appetite for sex and money propelled him through scandal after scandal. In 1903, the unexplained disappearance of his latest inamorata, excited public speculation. Would Miss Holland's whereabouts be discovered? And who, if anyone, would be held to account for her disappearance?

978 0 7524 6629 3

Visit our website and discover thousands of other History Press books.

www.thehistorypress.co.uk

The History Press